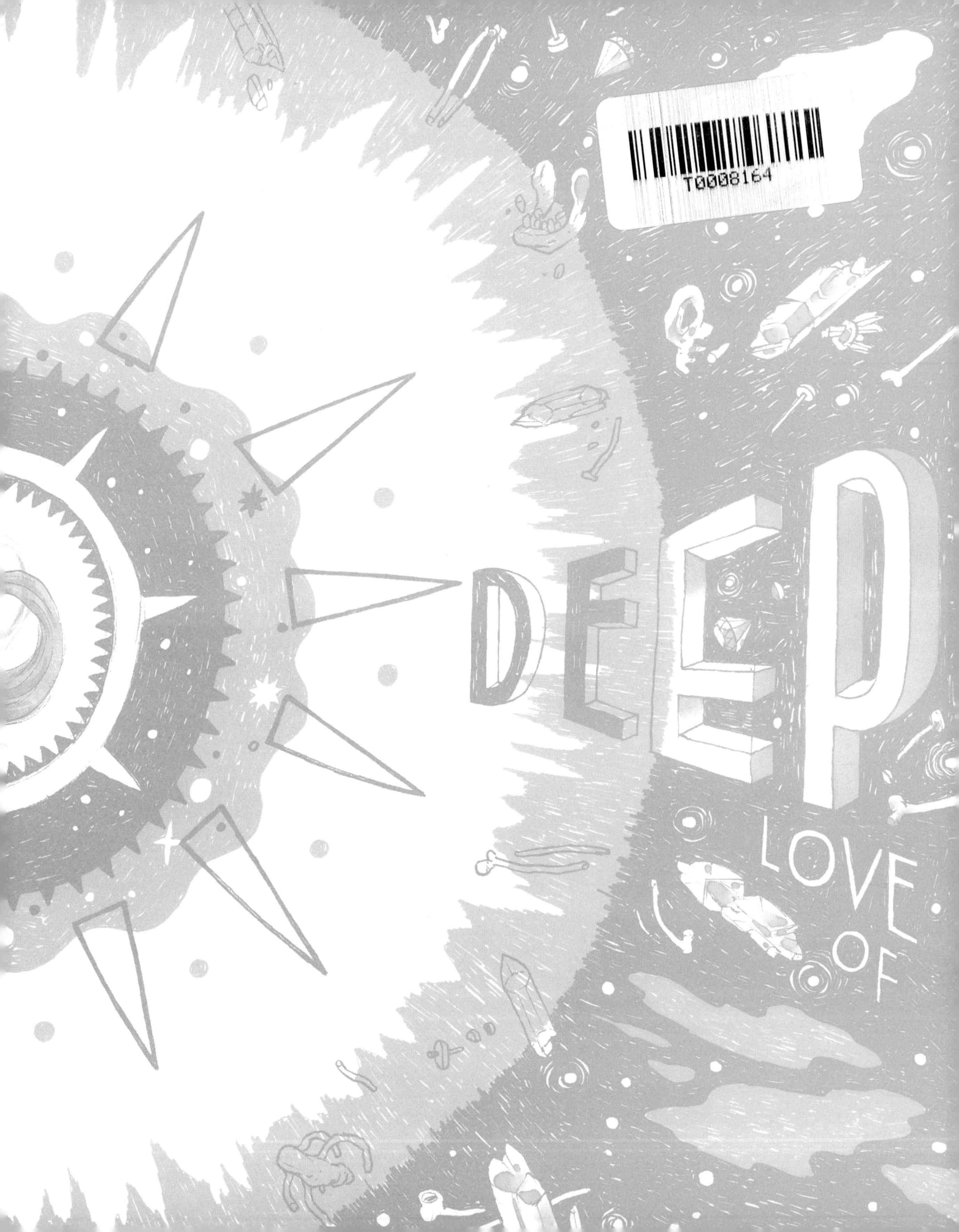

DEEP

LOVE

OF

I am going away,
and I am coming back to you.

JOHN 14:28

THE HOLY GHOST

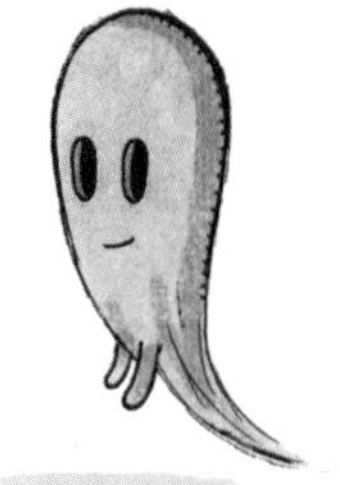

A SPIRITED COMIC

JOHN HENDRIX

ABRAMS COMICARTS
NEW YORK

OK, SO PERHAPS I MISUNDERSTOOD WHEN HE SAID "SEND THE COMFORTER."

IN SPIRIT

PATRICK McDONNELL

John Hendrix's *The Holy Ghost* is my type of comic strip: quiet, playful, comforting, and thoughtful. The art is beautiful to look at, with lots of space. Thus, stillness. As in all good comics, John's characters have that magical feeling of being alive on the page. His cast is endearing, drawn with love and care. Charles Schulz called this artistic quality "warmth." John has that here.

And to think of the Holy Ghost—why has no one ever come up with this idea before? John has created an ideal comic-strip character, someone who is ever present and sees the world from a unique and interesting perspective. Who wouldn't want to spend time with a friendly Holy Ghost?

The strip reminds me of a somewhat obscure, esoteric comic collection I discovered while in high school: *Zen Comics* by Ioanna Salajan. Her strip, about an old Buddhist monk's teachings to his young student, made a lasting impression on me. *Zen Comics* was different from any other comic I had read before, philosophical but totally charming and intriguing. Somehow it all worked. *The Holy Ghost* follows in those sandaled footsteps.

I'm not the guy who can delve deeply into the religious aspects of John's work, but I truly appreciate the spiritual angle of his strip. Comic strips are a perfect medium for the exploration and expression of simple truths. The short form, with its brevity and simplicity, is akin to such spiritual teachings as parables, sutras, and Zen koans.

And, like poetry, comic strips can cut to the chase and get to the heart of the matter with just a few words (and pictures). A good comic strip can be like a little prayer offered to the reader. With *The Holy Ghost*, John doesn't necessarily provide us with answers but instead poses some good questions. Big questions conveyed with humor and kindness. Questions invoked by a talking squirrel, a passionate badger, and a bright-blue Holy Ghost.

The Holy Ghost is about the mystery of it all.
My type of comic.

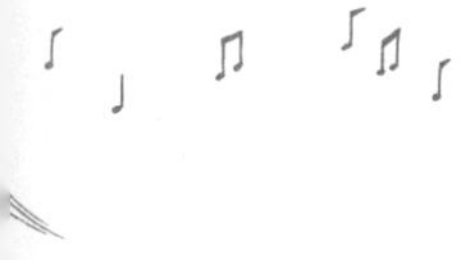

THE HOLY GHOST

WELL. IT IS A WORKABLE DRAFT, I GUESS.

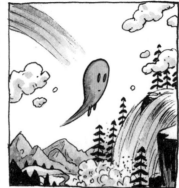

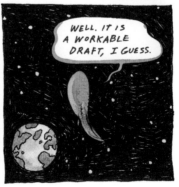

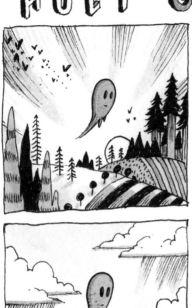

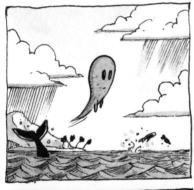

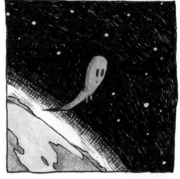

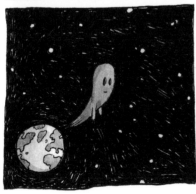

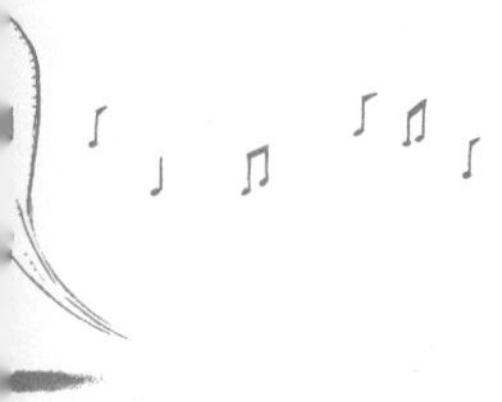

THE HOLY GHOST

I'M NOT FULFILLED.
-UGH-
SHOVE
AAAAAAAAAAA
AAAAAAAAA
AAAAA
CATCH
FEEL BETTER?

THE HOLY GHOST

SO MANY TODAY...
HELP US
LORD
PLEASE
MERCY
OH, GOD
GOD
PLEASE LORD
HELP
GOD
JESUS
OH LORD, HAVE MERCY
HAVE MERCY...
HELP
LORD, HELP
PLEASE GOD
HELP
GOD, HELP US...
O, PLEASE
OH... GOD
LORD
JESUS

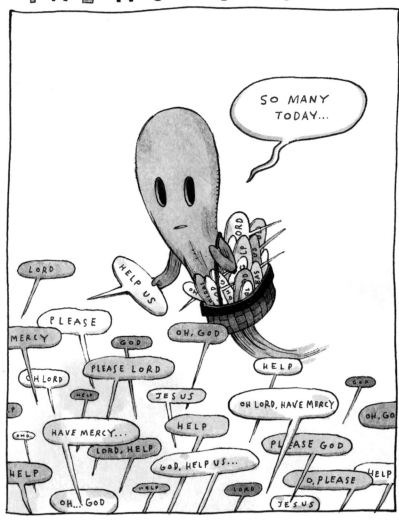

THE HOLY GHOST

I'M TIRED.
THIS IS STUPID.
I KNOW YOU'RE JUST
MAKE-BELIEVE... BUT
I'M ALONE. I NEED HELP...
BUT, YOU DON'T EXIST...
YOU... DON'T... EXIST...
Z Z Z

THE·HOLY·GHOST

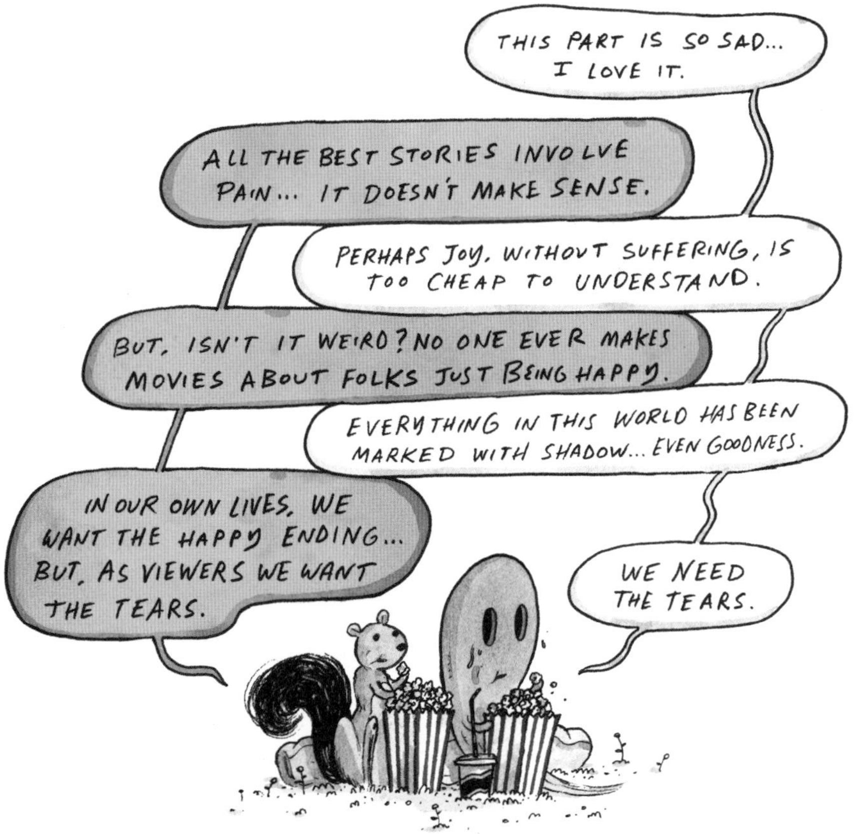
THIS PART IS SO SAD... I LOVE IT.
ALL THE BEST STORIES INVOLVE PAIN... IT DOESN'T MAKE SENSE.
PERHAPS JOY, WITHOUT SUFFERING, IS TOO CHEAP TO UNDERSTAND.
BUT, ISN'T IT WEIRD? NO ONE EVER MAKES MOVIES ABOUT FOLKS JUST BEING HAPPY.
EVERYTHING IN THIS WORLD HAS BEEN MARKED WITH SHADOW... EVEN GOODNESS.
IN OUR OWN LIVES, WE WANT THE HAPPY ENDING... BUT, AS VIEWERS WE WANT THE TEARS.
WE NEED THE TEARS.

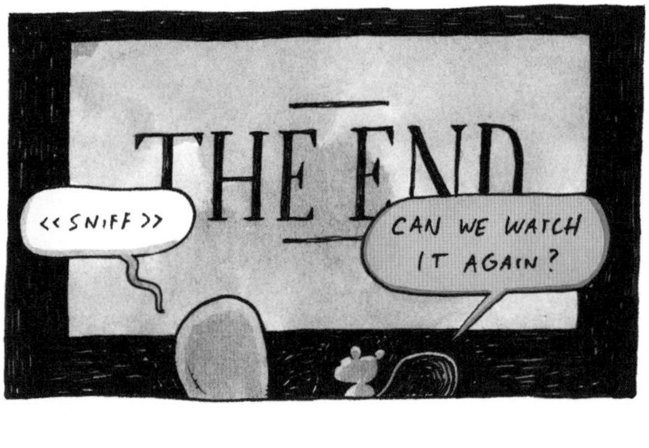
THE END
<< SNIFF >>
CAN WE WATCH IT AGAIN?

THE HOLY GHOST

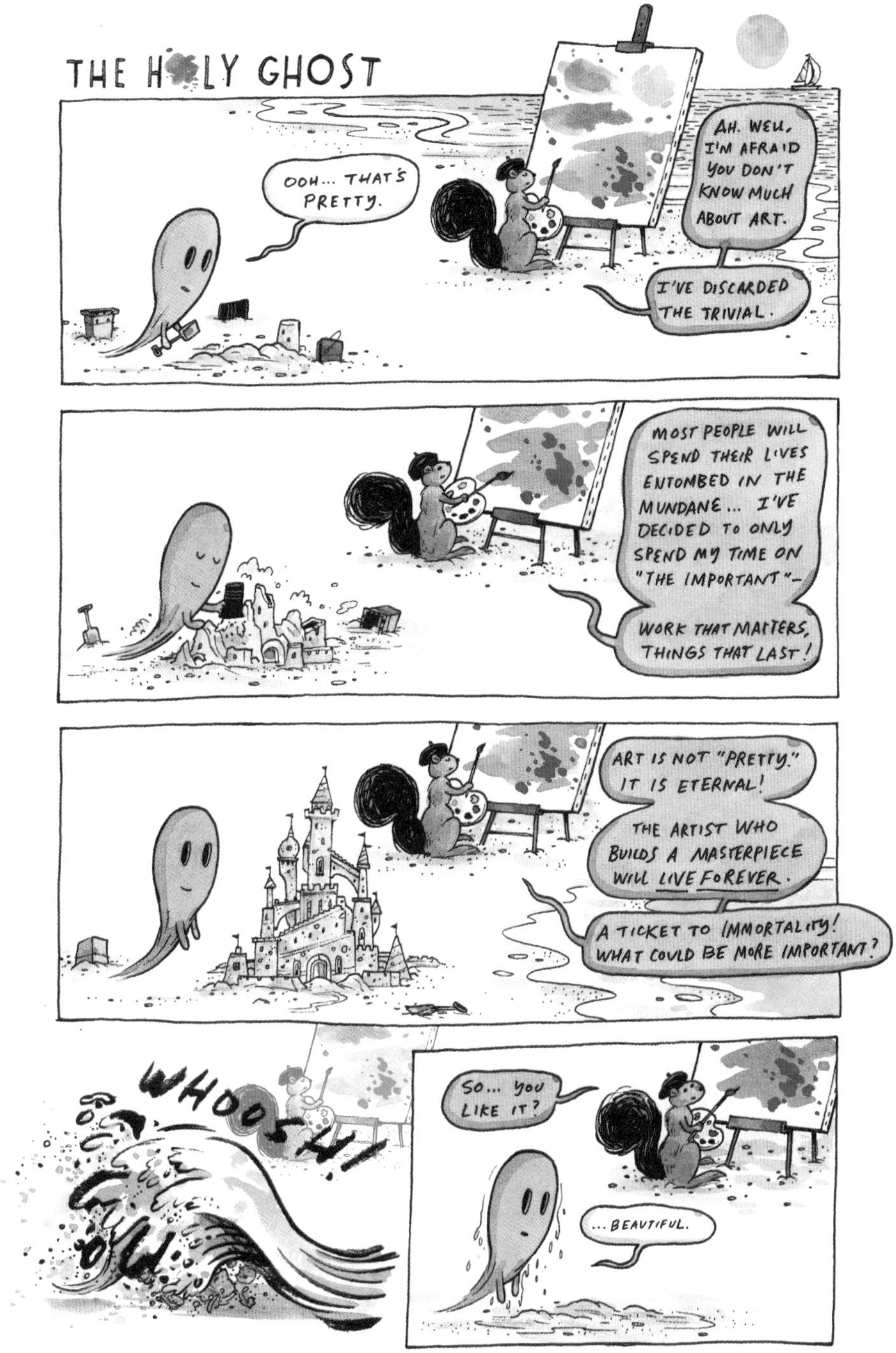

OOH... THAT'S PRETTY.
AH. WELL, I'M AFRAID YOU DON'T KNOW MUCH ABOUT ART.
I'VE DISCARDED THE TRIVIAL.
MOST PEOPLE WILL SPEND THEIR LIVES ENTOMBED IN THE MUNDANE... I'VE DECIDED TO ONLY SPEND MY TIME ON "THE IMPORTANT"—
WORK THAT MATTERS, THINGS THAT LAST!
ART IS NOT "PRETTY." IT IS ETERNAL!
THE ARTIST WHO BUILDS A MASTERPIECE WILL LIVE FOREVER.
A TICKET TO IMMORTALITY! WHAT COULD BE MORE IMPORTANT?
WHOOSH!
SO... YOU LIKE IT?
...BEAUTIFUL.

THE · HOLY · GHOST

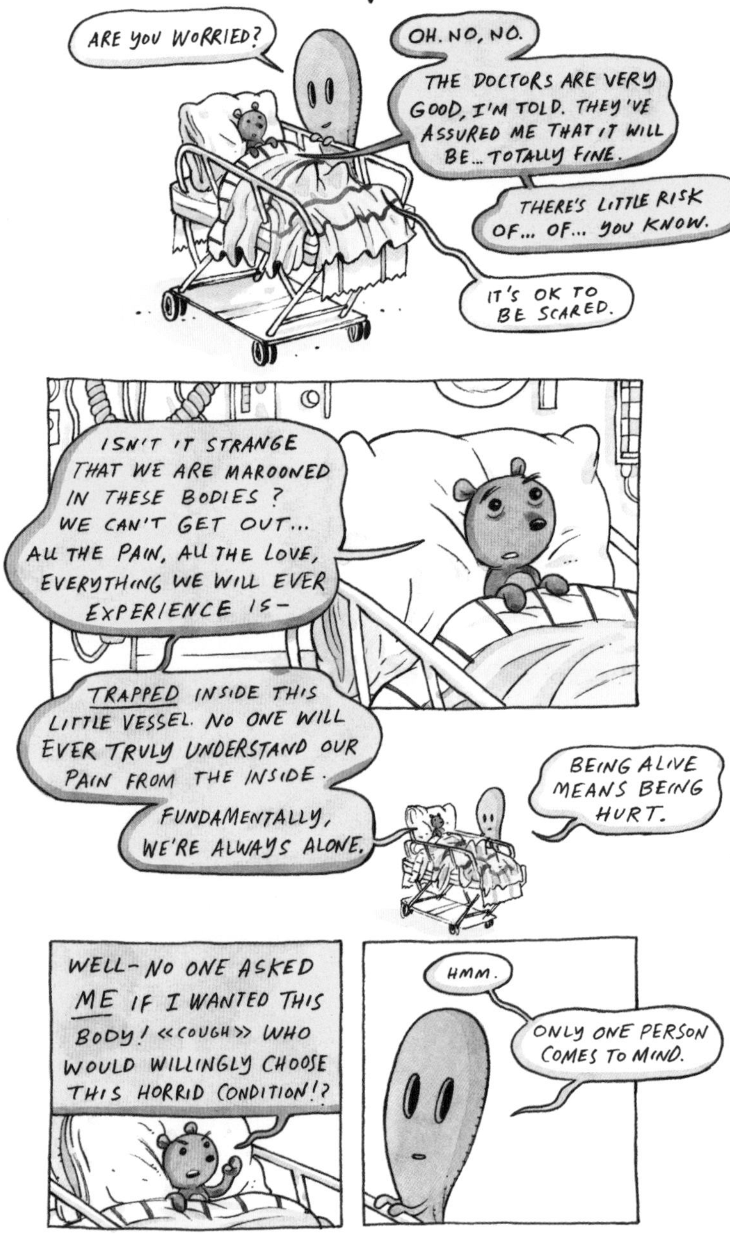
ARE YOU WORRIED?
OH. NO, NO.
THE DOCTORS ARE VERY GOOD, I'M TOLD. THEY'VE ASSURED ME THAT IT WILL BE... TOTALLY FINE.
THERE'S LITTLE RISK OF... OF... YOU KNOW.
IT'S OK TO BE SCARED.
ISN'T IT STRANGE THAT WE ARE MAROONED IN THESE BODIES? WE CAN'T GET OUT... ALL THE PAIN, ALL THE LOVE, EVERYTHING WE WILL EVER EXPERIENCE IS—
TRAPPED INSIDE THIS LITTLE VESSEL. NO ONE WILL EVER TRULY UNDERSTAND OUR PAIN FROM THE INSIDE.
FUNDAMENTALLY, WE'RE ALWAYS ALONE.
BEING ALIVE MEANS BEING HURT.
WELL— NO ONE ASKED ME IF I WANTED THIS BODY! «COUGH» WHO WOULD WILLINGLY CHOOSE THIS HORRID CONDITION!?
HMM.
ONLY ONE PERSON COMES TO MIND.

THE HOLY GHOST

REPENT
REPENT!
REPENT
GOD ONLY BLESSES THOSE WHO BLESS HIM!
REPENT
AHEM.
GOD'S MERCY IS THIS: "HE SENDS THE RAIN TO FALL ON THE JUST... AND ON THE UNJUST."
REPENT
WHICH AM I?!

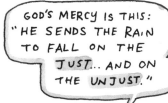

THE HOLY GHOST

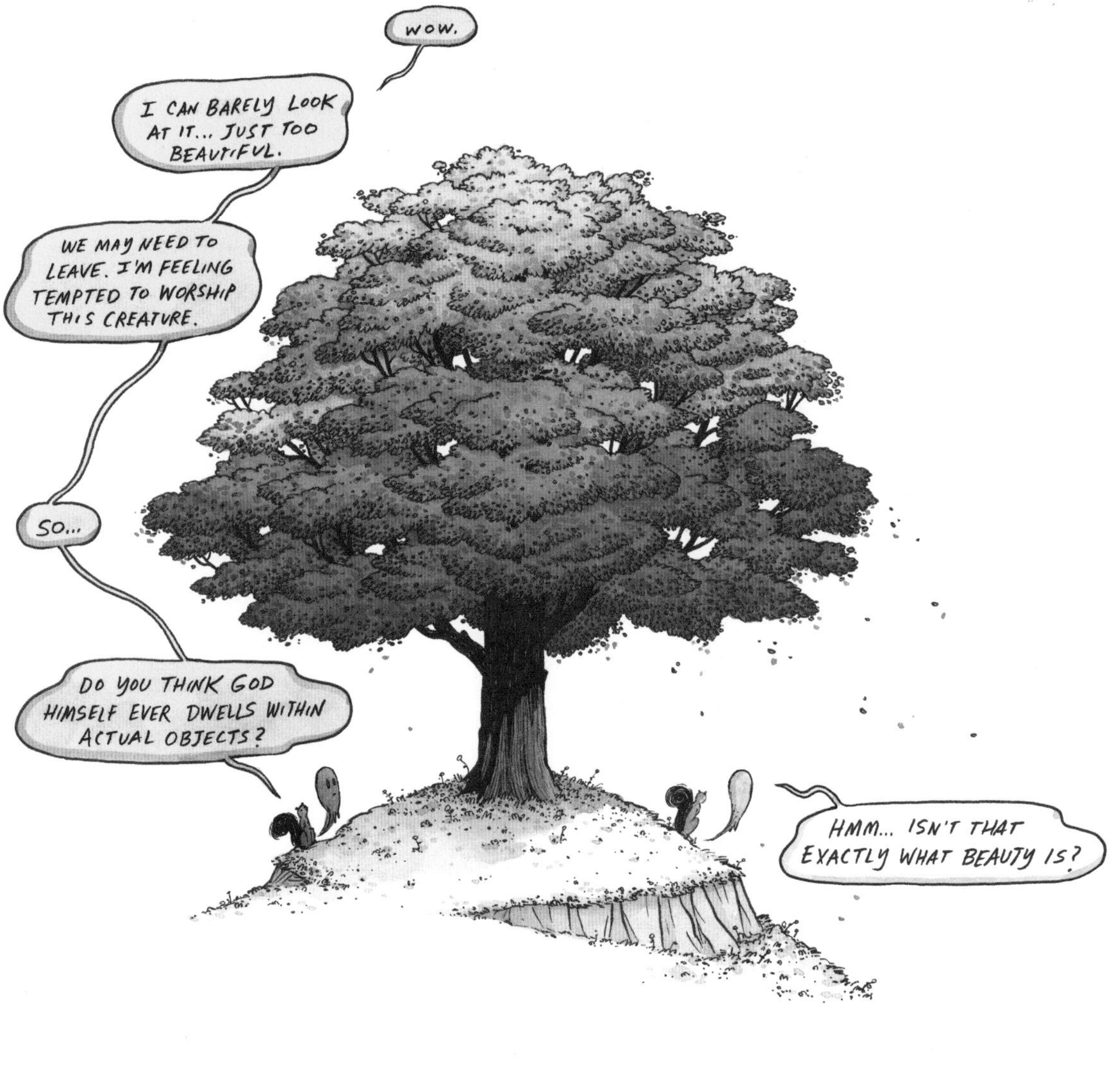
WOW.
I CAN BARELY LOOK AT IT... JUST TOO BEAUTIFUL.
WE MAY NEED TO LEAVE. I'M FEELING TEMPTED TO WORSHIP THIS CREATURE.
SO...
DO YOU THINK GOD HIMSELF EVER DWELLS WITHIN ACTUAL OBJECTS?
HMM... ISN'T THAT EXACTLY WHAT BEAUTY IS?

THE HOLY GHOST

WHICH IS HARDER TO ACCEPT: THAT EVERYTHING IS POINTLESS, OR THAT ALL ACTION AND THOUGHT IN THE UNIVERSE IS OF ETERNAL VALUE TO GOD...

I WANT EVERYTHING TO MATTER. I FEEL LIKE I'M... IMPORTANT FOR SOME REASON. BUT, SO MUCH AROUND ME FEELS... LIKE FUTILITY, RATHER THAN PURPOSE!

HMM...

WHICH IS HARDER TO BELIEVE: THAT GOD IS SURPRISED YOU FEEL THIS CONFLICT... OR THAT THE DOUBTS ARE BY DESIGN?

THE HOLY GHOST.

GAH! THESE DINGBATS ON THE "ACORN COUNCIL" ARE ALL CORRUPT AND... EVIL!

ARE THEY REALLY THAT BAD?

HOW CAN YOU BE SO NAÏVE, SO GULLIBLE, THAT YOU THINK THE BEST OF EVERYONE?

WHEN WAS THE LAST TIME YOU'VE ADMITTED TO BEING WRONG ON SOMETHING YOU BELIEVED?

OH, PLEASE—

I'M THE KIND OF PERSON WHO PRIDES THEMSELVES ON BEING VERY OPEN-MINDED.

HONESTLY, ARE YOU STILL CAPABLE OF CHANGING YOUR MIND? IS IT POSSIBLE THAT GOD MIGHT DISAGREE WITH ANY OF YOUR CONCLUSIONS?

GOD!?

HOW WILL YOU EVER KNOW IF YOUR "BELIEFS" CONSTRAIN YOUR ACTIONS— OR IF YOUR DESIRES BEND YOUR ETHICS?

OK—LISTEN, NO ONE IS PERFECT—

BUT IN THIS SPECIFIC CASE, I'M DEFINITELY RIGHT.

THE HOLY GHOST

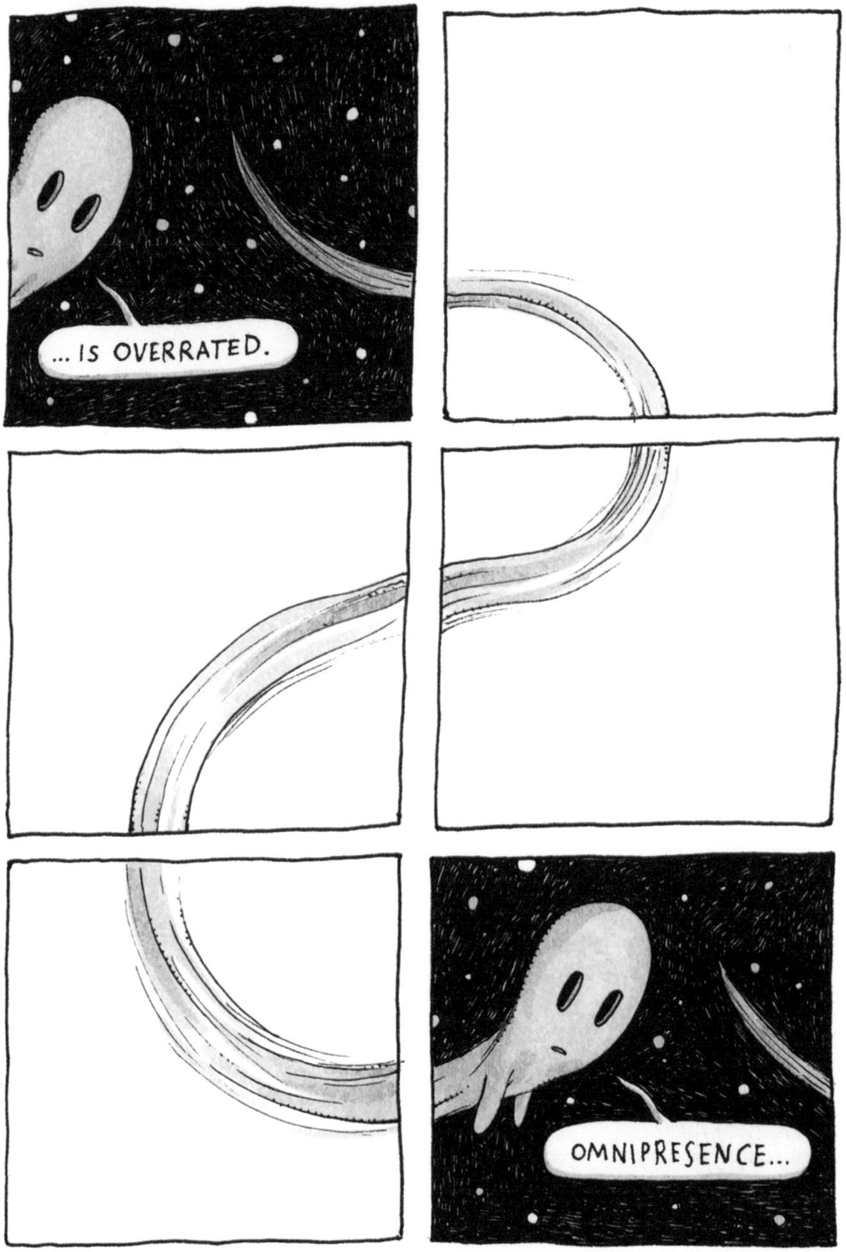
...IS OVERRATED.
OMNIPRESENCE...

THE HOLY GHOST

THANK YOU, LORD, FOR BLESSING ME...
THIS TREE IS A GIFT FROM YOU
I FEEL I'VE DONE ENOUGH TO PROVE I'LL USE THIS GIFT RESPONSIBLY - BUT - LORD,
"DO WITH IT AS YOU SEE FIT"
WELL, CRAP.

THE HOLY GHOST

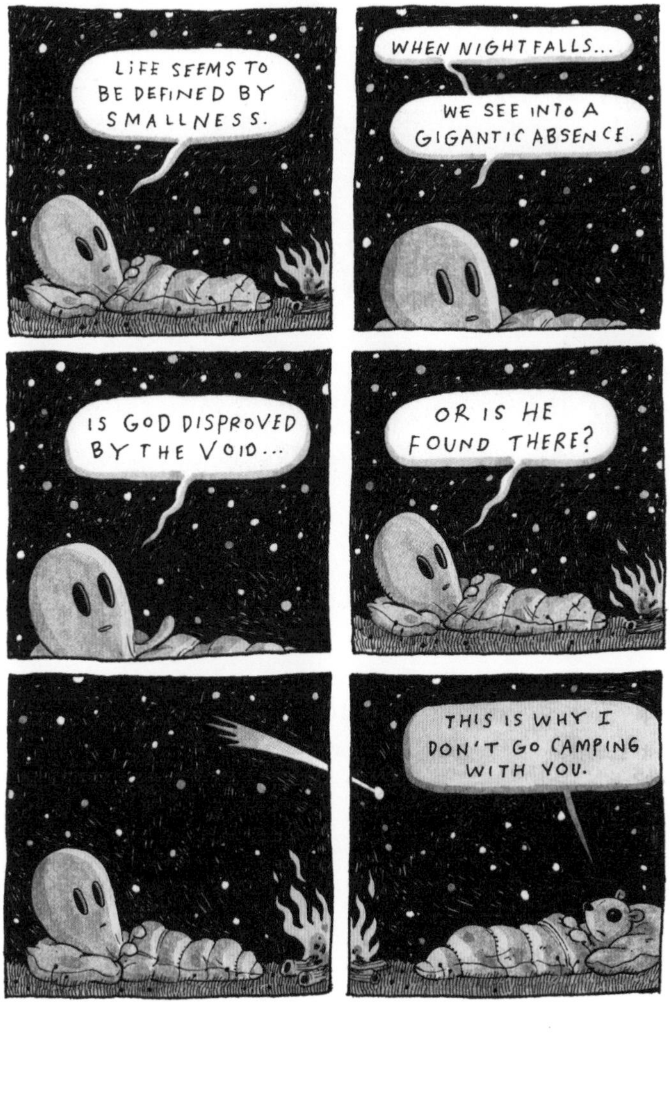
LIFE SEEMS TO BE DEFINED BY SMALLNESS.
WHEN NIGHTFALLS...
WE SEE INTO A GIGANTIC ABSENCE.
IS GOD DISPROVED BY THE VOID...
OR IS HE FOUND THERE?
THIS IS WHY I DON'T GO CAMPING WITH YOU.

THE HOLY GHOST

THERE IS NO GOD!
OH YEAH!?
"PROVE IT!!!"
GOD IS REAL!
I'VE MADE LUNCH. WOULD EITHER OF YOU LIKE A RED-HERRING SANDWICH?

THE HOLY GHOST

LOOK AT THIS HORRIBLE THING.
AH, YES...
IT IS A PARASITIC WASP. SHE LAYS HUNDREDS OF EGGS INSIDE THE CATERPILLAR'S BODY. AS THE EGGS HATCH, THE LARVAE EAT THEIR WAY OUT OF THE HOST'S BODY, USING IT AS FOOD. GOD MADE IT ON THE FIFTH DAY.
UGH.
GOD IS A MONSTER.
WELL, HE MADE KITTIES RIGHT AFTER TO BALANCE THINGS OUT.

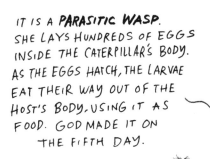

THE HOLY GHOST

DID YOU KNOW IT'S NOW BEEN POSITED BY SCIENCE THAT THERE IS A 90% CHANCE WE ARE LIVING INSIDE A VAST SIMULATION?

MMM.

SURE. THINK ABOUT IT—TECHNOLOGY IMPROVES EXPONENTIALLY. HOW CAN WE KNOW FOR SURE THAT THIS ISN'T JUST A DIGITAL ZOO CURATED BY ALIEN BEINGS?

GOD IS FINALLY IRRELEVANT. THERE IS NO HIGHER POWER BEYOND TECHNOLOGY!

HUH.

DON'T YOU SEE? IF THIS IS ALL DESIGNED FOR US, THEN THERE MUST BE A PURPOSE. THERE MUST BE A TRUE MEANING TO LIFE!

OH REALLY?

WHY WOULD SOME GREAT INTELLIGENCE MAKE SUCH A VAST, INTRICATE, AND EXPENSIVE BOX OF WONDERS— EXCLUSIVELY FOR OUR EXPERIENCE... FOR NO REASON!

I THINK YOU ARE ON TO SOMETHING.

HOLD ON. I NEED A REBOOT.

INDEED.

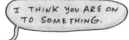

THE HOLY GHOST

HEY—YOU OK?
YES, I'M FINE. JUST TAKING REASONABLE PRECAUTIONS.
IT IS A VERY DANGEROUS WORLD... YOU CAN NEVER BE TOO SAFE.
YOU SEE, EVERYTHING STARTS WITH PERSONAL THRIVING...
SO, YOU DON'T WANT TO HIT THE BALL AROUND?
NO, THE WORLD NEEDS ME TO BE AT 100%, MENTALLY AND PHYSICALLY.
LOOK, YOUR NEED FOR NONPRODUCTIVE ACTIVITY IS CHARMING... BUT I JUST CAN'T RISK WASTING MY POTENTIAL.
I'M PRESERVING MYSELF FOR SOMETHING GREAT! AND UNTIL THEN, I CAN'T EXPOSE MYSELF TO ANY PAIN OR ILLNESS...
NO CHOICE THAT PUTS MY GIFTS IN DANGER IS WORTH IT!
SO, HOW LONG HAVE YOU BEEN IN THERE?
THREE DAYS.
DOES IT SMELL BAD IN THERE?
IT IS TRULY UNBEARABLE.

THE HOLY GHOST

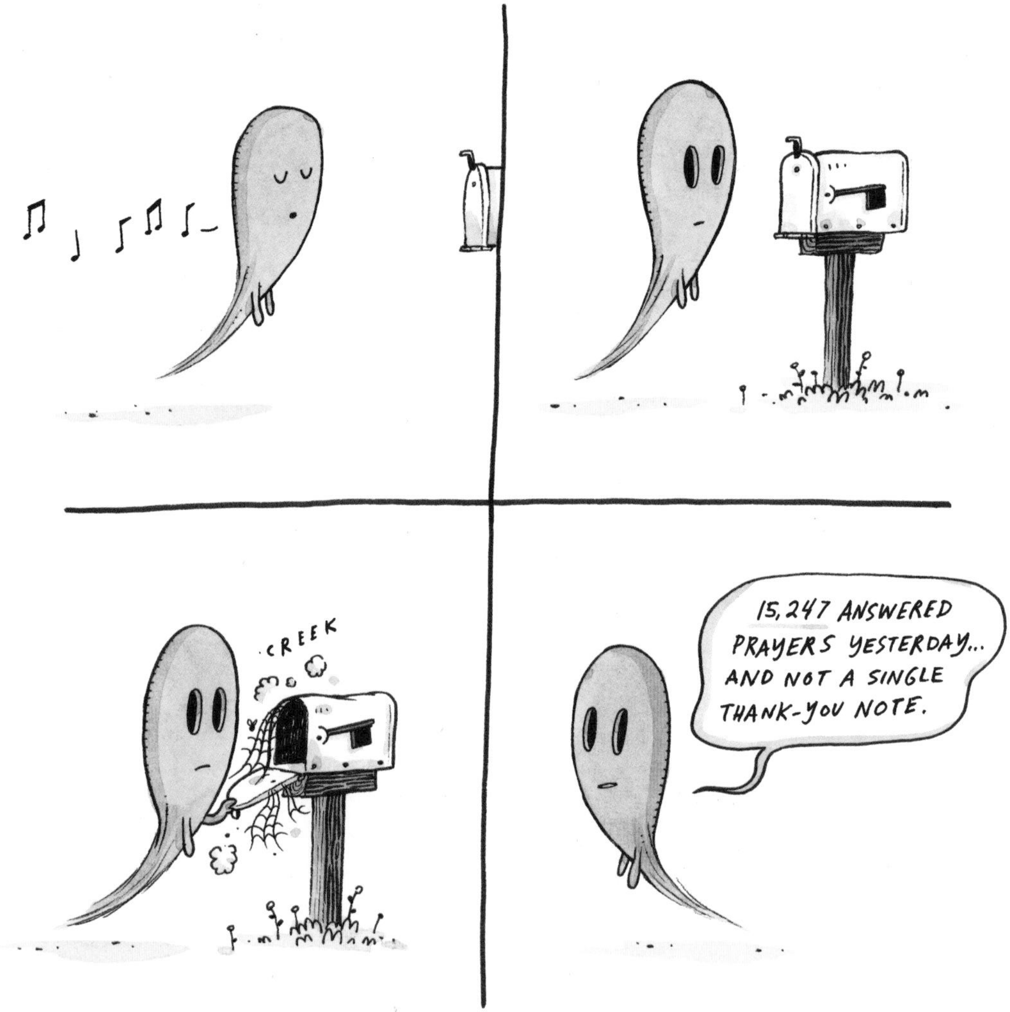
CREEK
15,247 ANSWERED PRAYERS YESTERDAY... AND NOT A SINGLE THANK-YOU NOTE.

THE HOLY GHOST

MARION!
—DON'T LOOKAT IT!
—KEEP YOUR EYES SHUT!
IT'S—BEAUTIFUL—
SKA-BLOOSH!
CLICK
SKA-BLOOSH

THE HOLY GHOST

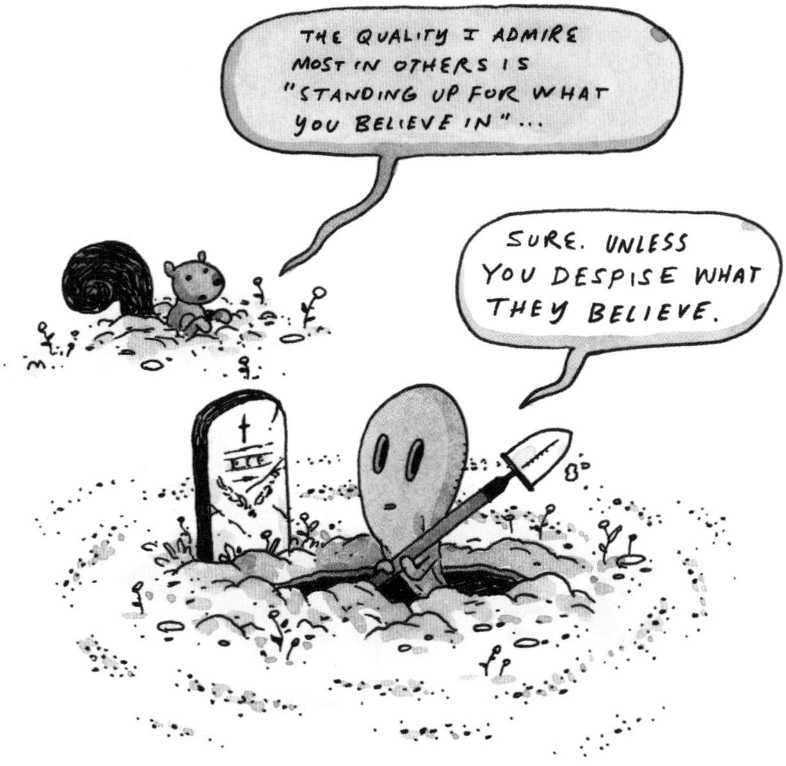

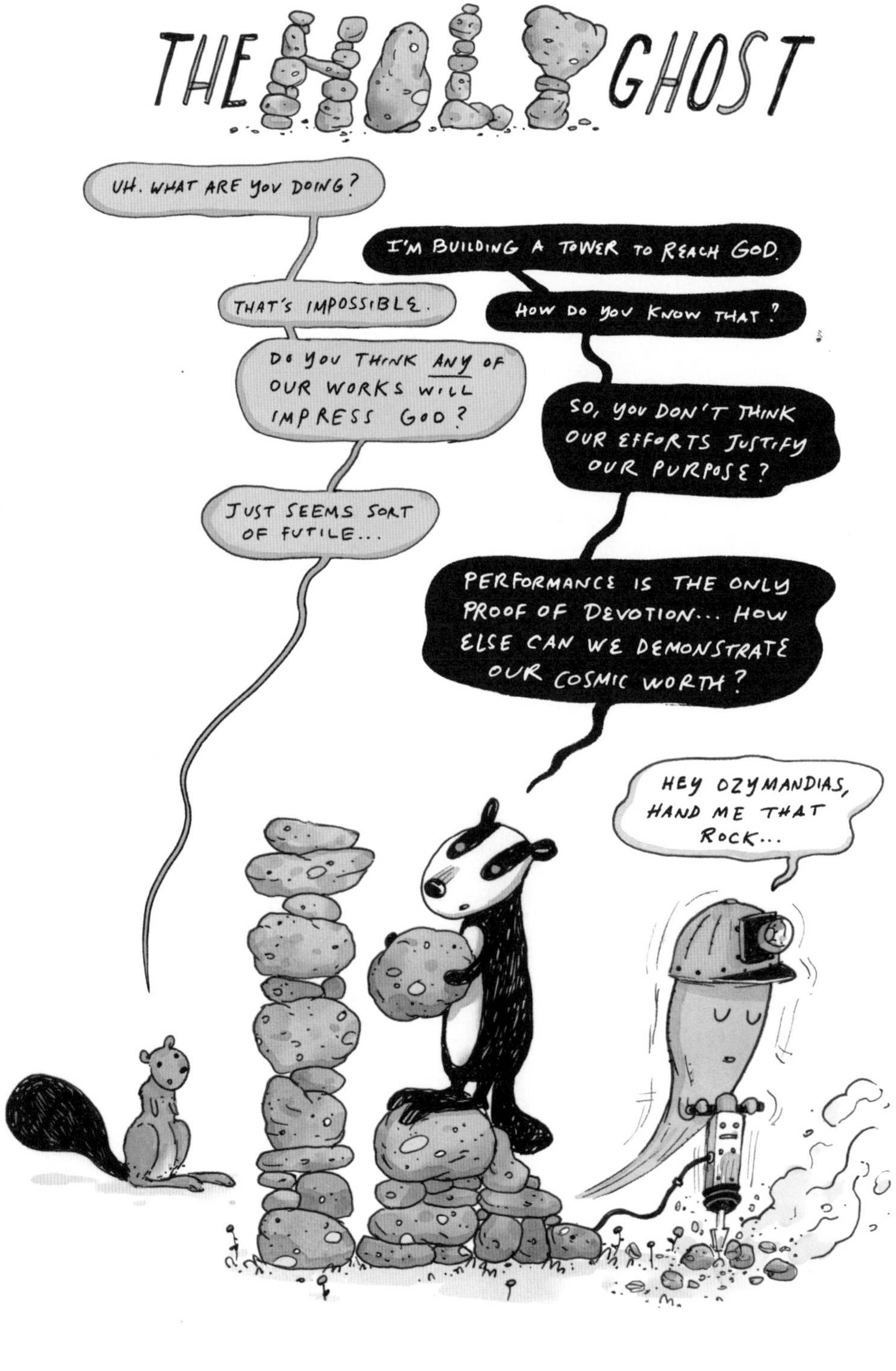
THE HOLY GHOST
UH. WHAT ARE YOU DOING?
I'M BUILDING A TOWER TO REACH GOD.
THAT'S IMPOSSIBLE.
HOW DO YOU KNOW THAT?
DO YOU THINK ANY OF OUR WORKS WILL IMPRESS GOD?
SO, YOU DON'T THINK OUR EFFORTS JUSTIFY OUR PURPOSE?
JUST SEEMS SORT OF FUTILE...
PERFORMANCE IS THE ONLY PROOF OF DEVOTION... HOW ELSE CAN WE DEMONSTRATE OUR COSMIC WORTH?
HEY OZYMANDIAS, HAND ME THAT ROCK...

THE HOLY GHOST

I LOVE DUMPSTER DIVING.

WHOA. THAT'S A LOT OF CRUTCHES.

HEH. I GUESS LOTSA FOLKS WERE HEALED, EH?

THE DAY IS COMING...

SWORDS WILL BE REMADE INTO PLOWSHARES—AND CRUTCHES WILL BE TURNED INTO KINDLING.

EVERYTHING SAD WILL BE REVERSED. FOREVER.

WELL, I'M TAKING THEM. UNTIL THEN...

PAIN IS A GROWTH INDUSTRY.

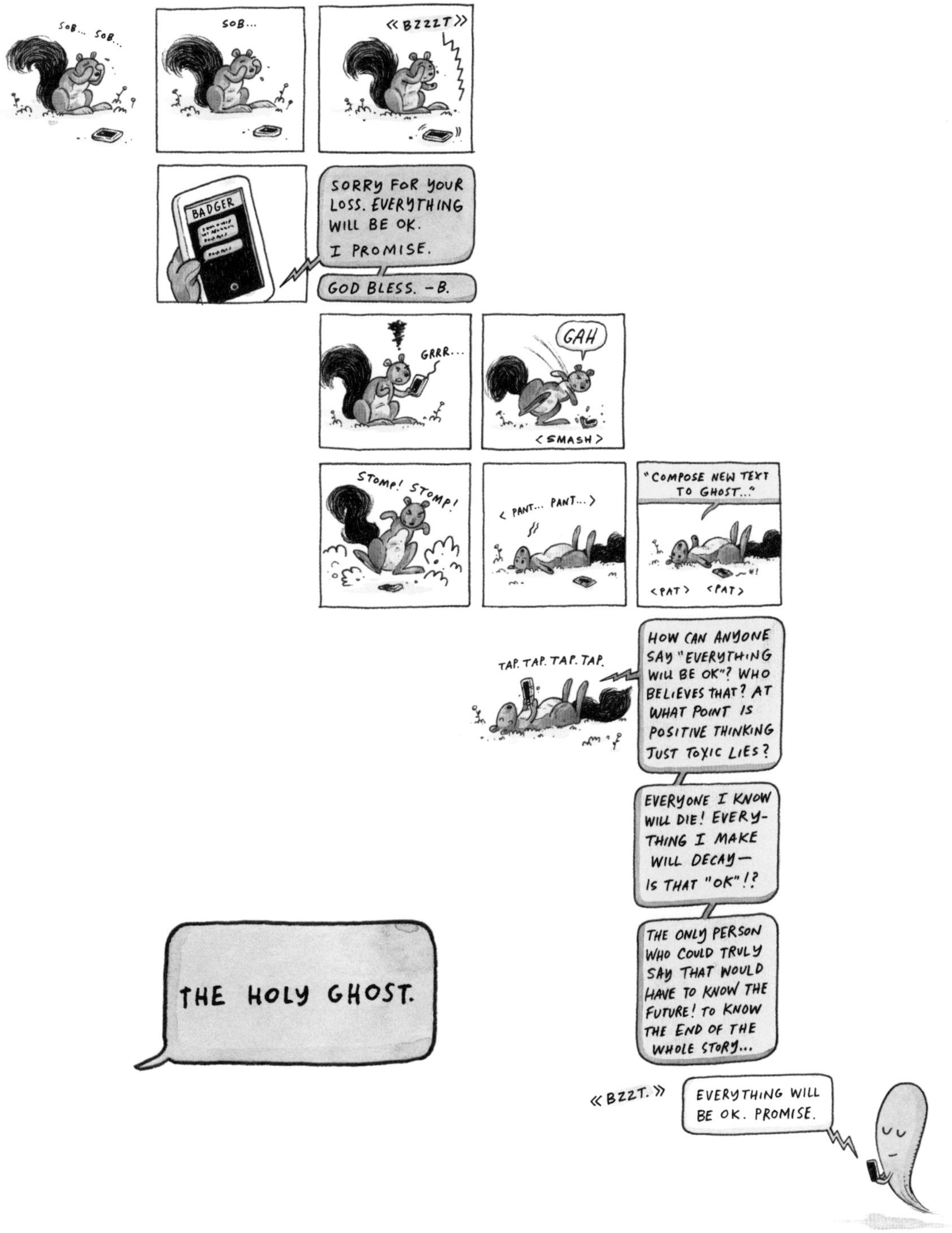
SOB... SOB...
SOB...
«BZZZT»
BADGER
SORRY FOR YOUR LOSS. EVERYTHING WILL BE OK. I PROMISE.
GOD BLESS. -B.
GRRR...
GAH
<SMASH>
STOMP! STOMP!
< PANT... PANT... >
"COMPOSE NEW TEXT TO GHOST..."
<PAT> <PAT>
TAP. TAP. TAP. TAP.
HOW CAN ANYONE SAY "EVERYTHING WILL BE OK"? WHO BELIEVES THAT? AT WHAT POINT IS POSITIVE THINKING JUST TOXIC LIES?
EVERYONE I KNOW WILL DIE! EVERY-THING I MAKE WILL DECAY— IS THAT "OK"!?
THE ONLY PERSON WHO COULD TRULY SAY THAT WOULD HAVE TO KNOW THE FUTURE! TO KNOW THE END OF THE WHOLE STORY...
THE HOLY GHOST.
«BZZT.»
EVERYTHING WILL BE OK. PROMISE.

THE HOLY GHOST
JESUS...
JESUS H. CHRIST ALMIGHTY! GOD!
OW.

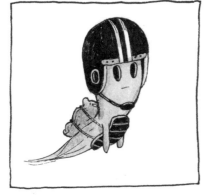

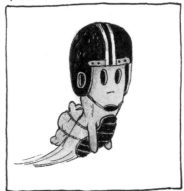

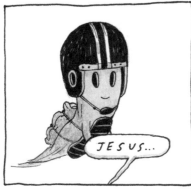

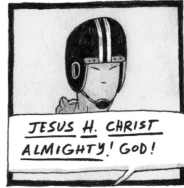

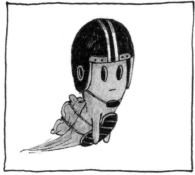

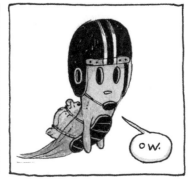

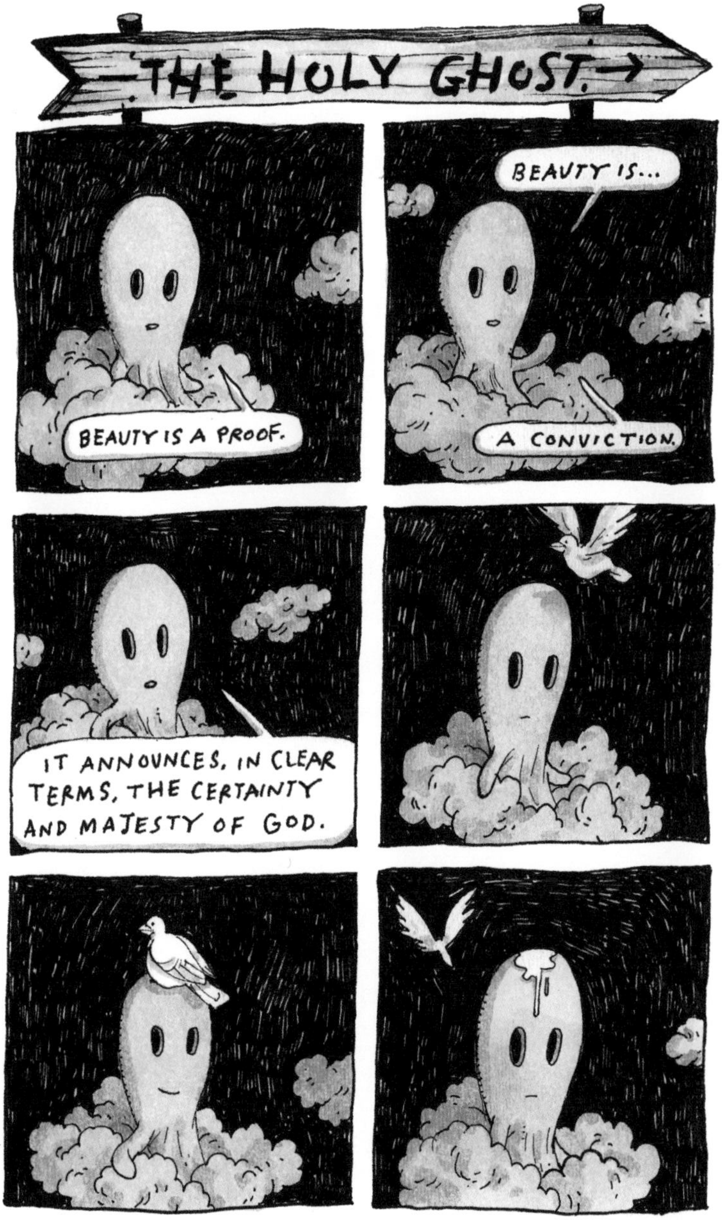
THE HOLY GHOST.
BEAUTY IS A PROOF.
BEAUTY IS...
A CONVICTION.
IT ANNOUNCES, IN CLEAR TERMS, THE CERTAINTY AND MAJESTY OF GOD.

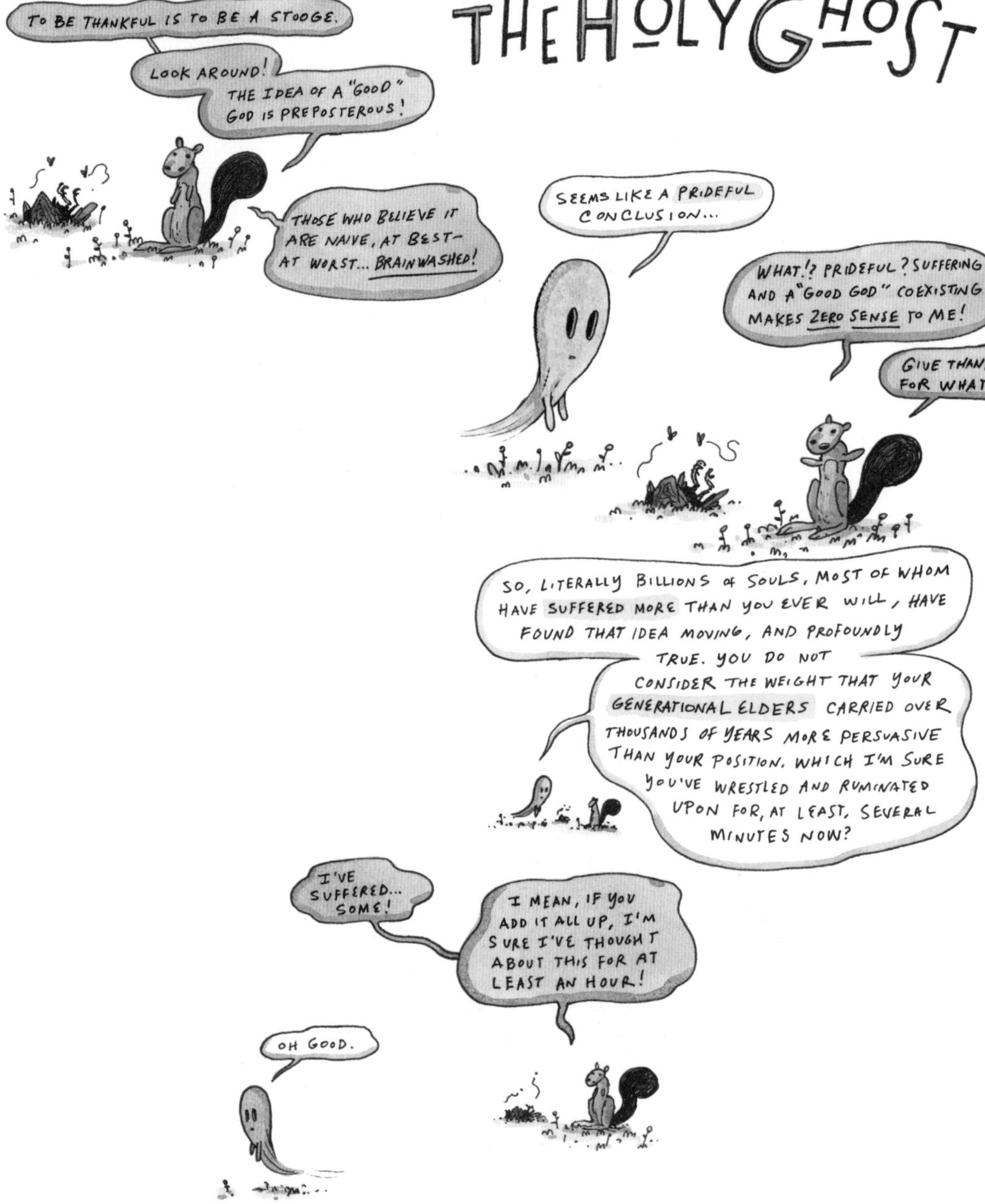
THE HOLY GHOST
TO BE THANKFUL IS TO BE A STOOGE.
LOOK AROUND! THE IDEA OF A "GOOD" GOD IS PREPOSTEROUS!
THOSE WHO BELIEVE IT ARE NAIVE, AT BEST- AT WORST... BRAINWASHED!
SEEMS LIKE A PRIDEFUL CONCLUSION...
WHAT!? PRIDEFUL? SUFFERING AND A "GOOD GOD" COEXISTING MAKES ZERO SENSE TO ME!
GIVE THANKS, FOR WHAT!?
SO, LITERALLY BILLIONS OF SOULS, MOST OF WHOM HAVE SUFFERED MORE THAN YOU EVER WILL, HAVE FOUND THAT IDEA MOVING, AND PROFOUNDLY TRUE. YOU DO NOT CONSIDER THE WEIGHT THAT YOUR GENERATIONAL ELDERS CARRIED OVER THOUSANDS OF YEARS MORE PERSUASIVE THAN YOUR POSITION, WHICH I'M SURE YOU'VE WRESTLED AND RUMINATED UPON FOR, AT LEAST, SEVERAL MINUTES NOW?
I'VE SUFFERED... SOME!
I MEAN, IF YOU ADD IT ALL UP, I'M SURE I'VE THOUGHT ABOUT THIS FOR AT LEAST AN HOUR!
OH GOOD.

THE HOLY GHOST

HEY! WHAT ARE YOU DOING?
WHO, ME?
UH, JUST THE USUAL
Bonk

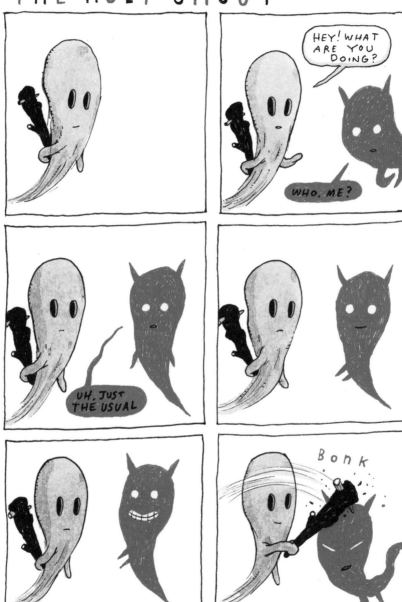

THE HOLY GHOST

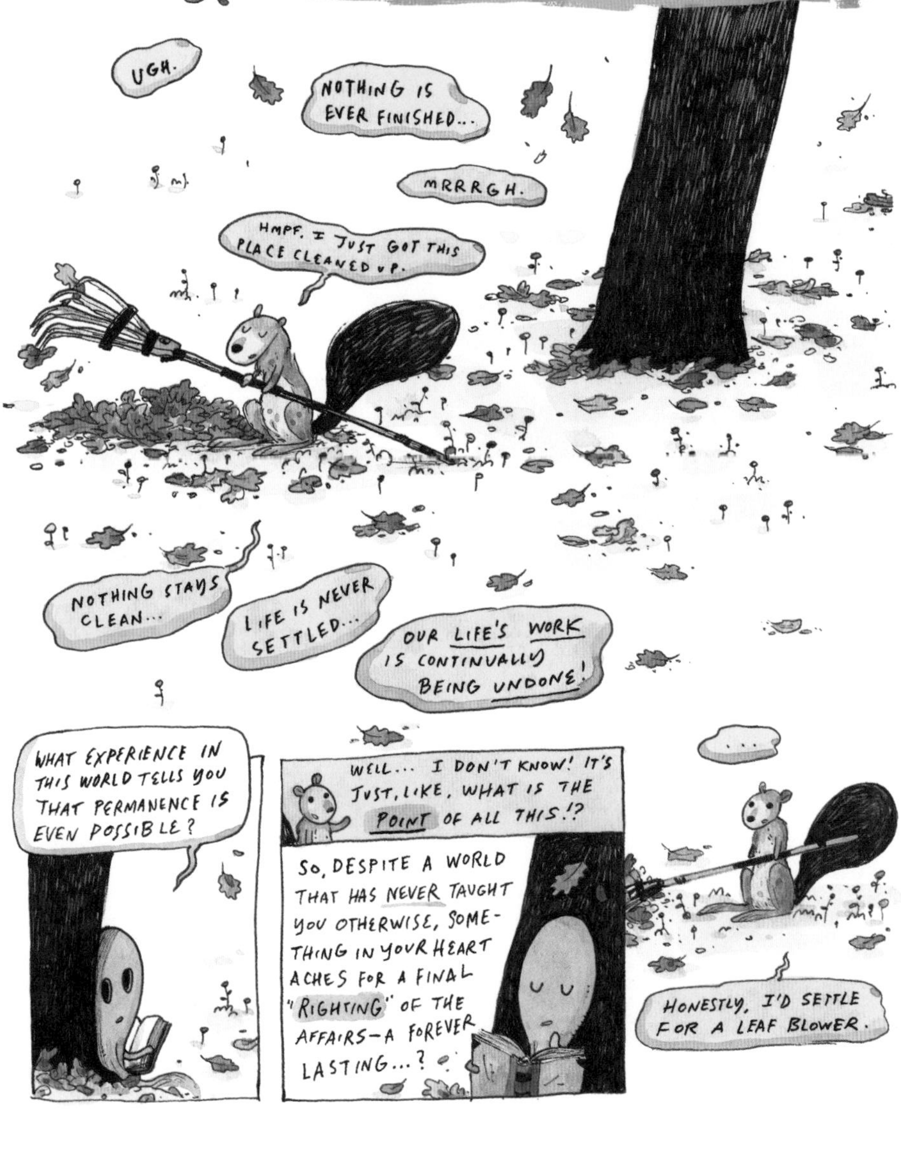
UGH.
NOTHING IS EVER FINISHED...
MRRRGH.
HMPF. I JUST GOT THIS PLACE CLEANED UP.
NOTHING STAYS CLEAN...
LIFE IS NEVER SETTLED...
OUR LIFE'S WORK IS CONTINUALLY BEING UNDONE!
WHAT EXPERIENCE IN THIS WORLD TELLS YOU THAT PERMANENCE IS EVEN POSSIBLE?
WELL... I DON'T KNOW! IT'S JUST, LIKE, WHAT IS THE POINT OF ALL THIS!?
SO, DESPITE A WORLD THAT HAS NEVER TAUGHT YOU OTHERWISE, SOMETHING IN YOUR HEART ACHES FOR A FINAL "RIGHTING" OF THE AFFAIRS—A FOREVER LASTING...?
...
HONESTLY, I'D SETTLE FOR A LEAF BLOWER.

THE HOLY GHOST

HAS GOD FORSAKEN ME?
SOB
SOB
NO.
SOB
HE IS PUNISHING ME FOR MY DOUBTS!!!
NO.
PAIN IS A SIGN OF DISOBEDIENCE.
NO.
WILL GOD EVER JUST SPEAK TO ME?
YES!

THE HOLY GHOST

SO, DO YOU THINK FOLKS ARE MOSTLY GOOD—

OR MOSTLY BAD?

NEARLY EVERYONE BELIEVES THEMSELVES TO BE "GOOD."

SMACK

BUT, WE CAN'T KNOW WHAT "GOOD" OR "BAD" IS IF WE DON'T KNOW YOUR PURPOSE.

MY PURPOSE?

IS A BASEBALL GOOD, OR BAD?

LIKE, WHAT DOES IT DO?

SMACK

NO. WHAT IS IT MADE FOR? NOT FUNCTION BUT PURPOSE. A BASEBALL IS A BAD TYPEWRITER, FOR INSTANCE, BUT IT IS A GREAT TOY.

IF WE CAN'T AGREE ON THE PURPOSE, WE CAN NEVER EVALUATE ITS GOODNESS!

HEH.

YOU'LL KNOW PRETTY QUICKLY ONCE I BEAN YOU WITH IT.

MORE ABOUT YOU THAN THE BALL.

THE HOLY GHOST

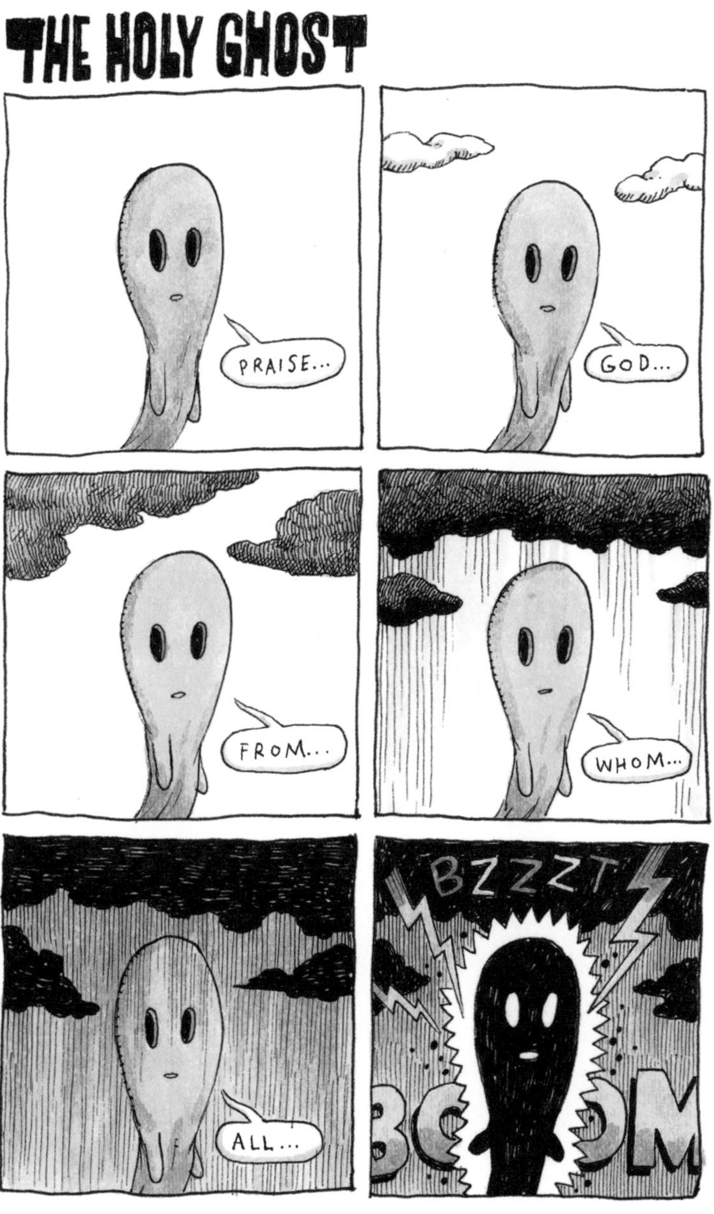
PRAISE...
GOD...
FROM...
WHOM...
ALL...
BZZZT

the Holy Ghost

WEEEEEE
EEEE
WHOOOOOOOOO
WEEEEEEEEEE

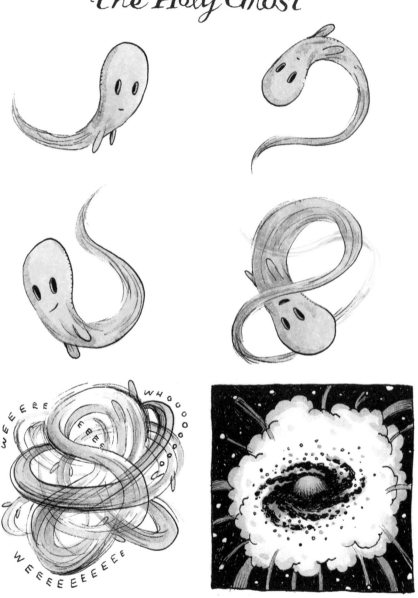

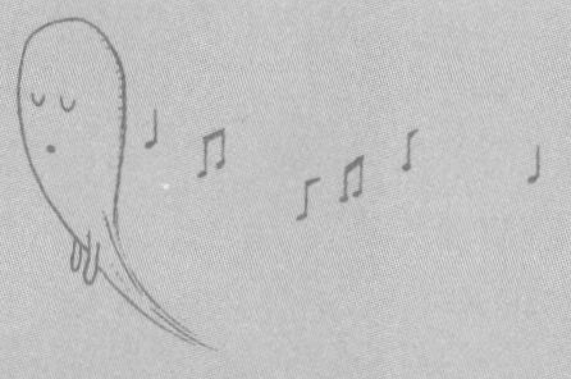

THE HOLY GHOST

FLIP
A POIGNANT, FLEETING BEAUTY THAT LEAVES A VAGUE RESIDUE OF SADNESS
SUMMER
WINTER
CLICK
POOF

the HOLY Ghost

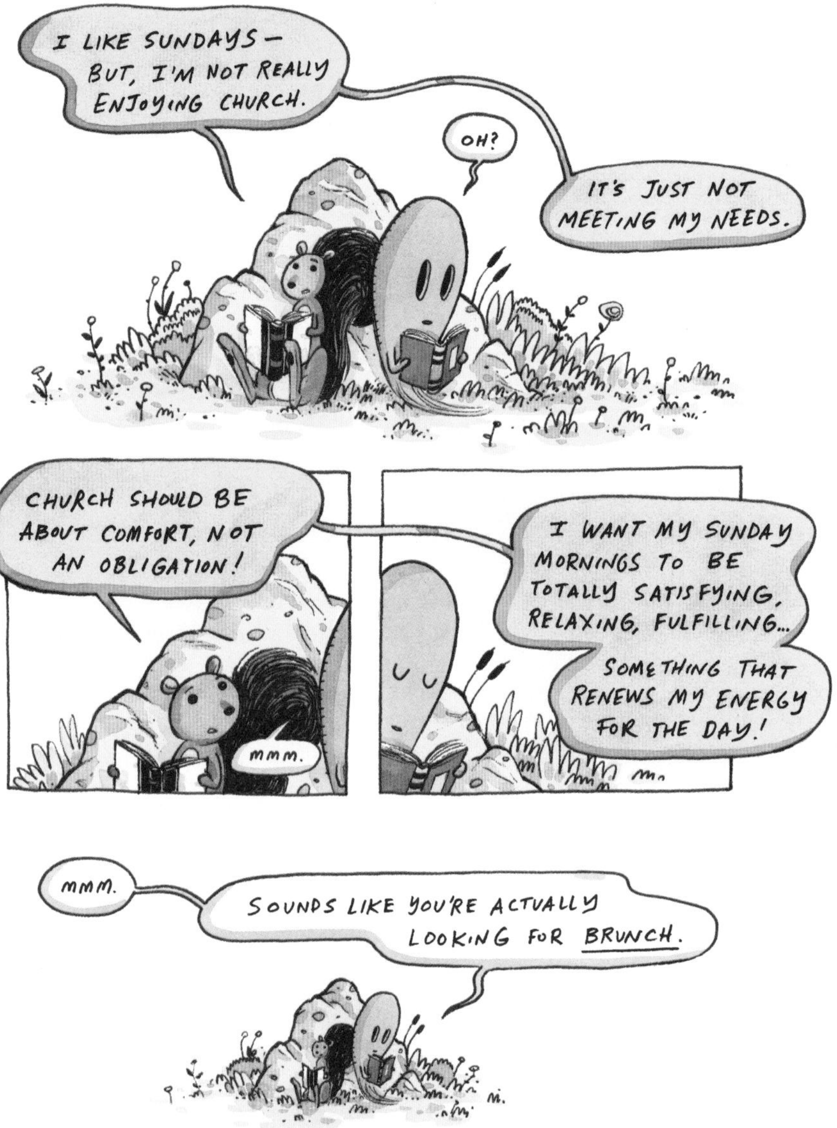
I LIKE SUNDAYS — BUT, I'M NOT REALLY ENJOYING CHURCH.
OH?
IT'S JUST NOT MEETING MY NEEDS.
CHURCH SHOULD BE ABOUT COMFORT, NOT AN OBLIGATION!
I WANT MY SUNDAY MORNINGS TO BE TOTALLY SATISFYING, RELAXING, FULFILLING...
SOMETHING THAT RENEWS MY ENERGY FOR THE DAY!
mmm.
mmm.
SOUNDS LIKE YOU'RE ACTUALLY LOOKING FOR BRUNCH.

THE HOLY GHOST

LORD, TODAY WE CELEBRATE BADGER NATION...
A DIVINE VESSEL OF YOUR WILL ON EARTH.

THOUGH WE LIVE IN AN AGE OF DARKNESS,
THE SUCCESS OF OUR
LAND IS PROOF THAT
THE LORD IS MANIFEST
IN OUR ACTIONS!
...
AS IT IS ONLY BY GOD ALONE,
THAT ANYTHING SUCCEEDS—
WE CAN BE CONFIDENT THAT
THE LORD IS ON OUR SIDE.
YOUR WILL AND BADGER NATION
ARE INSEPARABLE!!!

A-TEN-HUT!
SOUND OFF...

WHO IS THE AUTHOR OF OUR FAITH?

GOD ALONE!

ALL SOULS HAVE:

SINNED AND FALLEN SHORT OF THE GLORY OF GOD!

AND IF YOUR HAND CAUSES YOU TO SIN:

CUT IT OFF!!!

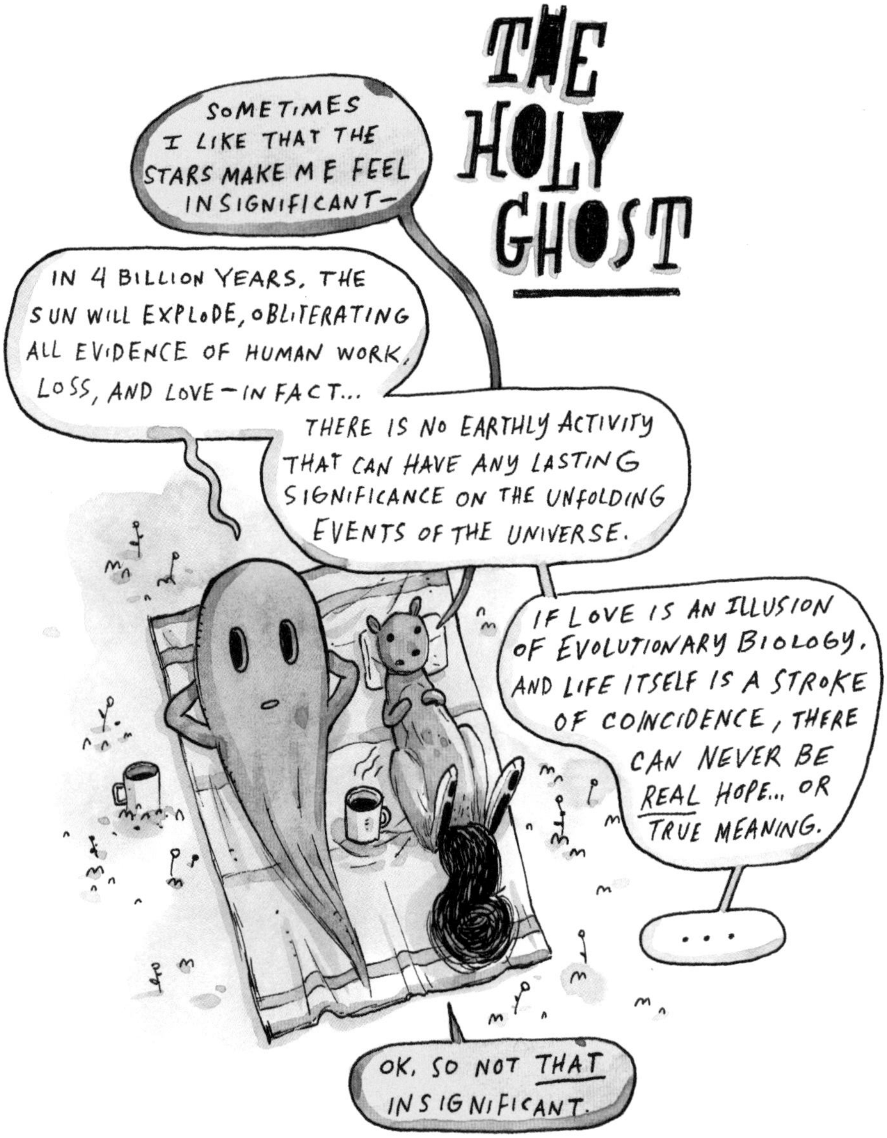
THE HOLY GHOST
SOMETIMES I LIKE THAT THE STARS MAKE ME FEEL INSIGNIFICANT—
IN 4 BILLION YEARS, THE SUN WILL EXPLODE, OBLITERATING ALL EVIDENCE OF HUMAN WORK, LOSS, AND LOVE—IN FACT...
THERE IS NO EARTHLY ACTIVITY THAT CAN HAVE ANY LASTING SIGNIFICANCE ON THE UNFOLDING EVENTS OF THE UNIVERSE.
IF LOVE IS AN ILLUSION OF EVOLUTIONARY BIOLOGY, AND LIFE ITSELF IS A STROKE OF COINCIDENCE, THERE CAN NEVER BE REAL HOPE... OR TRUE MEANING.
...
OK, SO NOT THAT INSIGNIFICANT.

T·H·E·H·O·L·Y·G·H·O·S·T

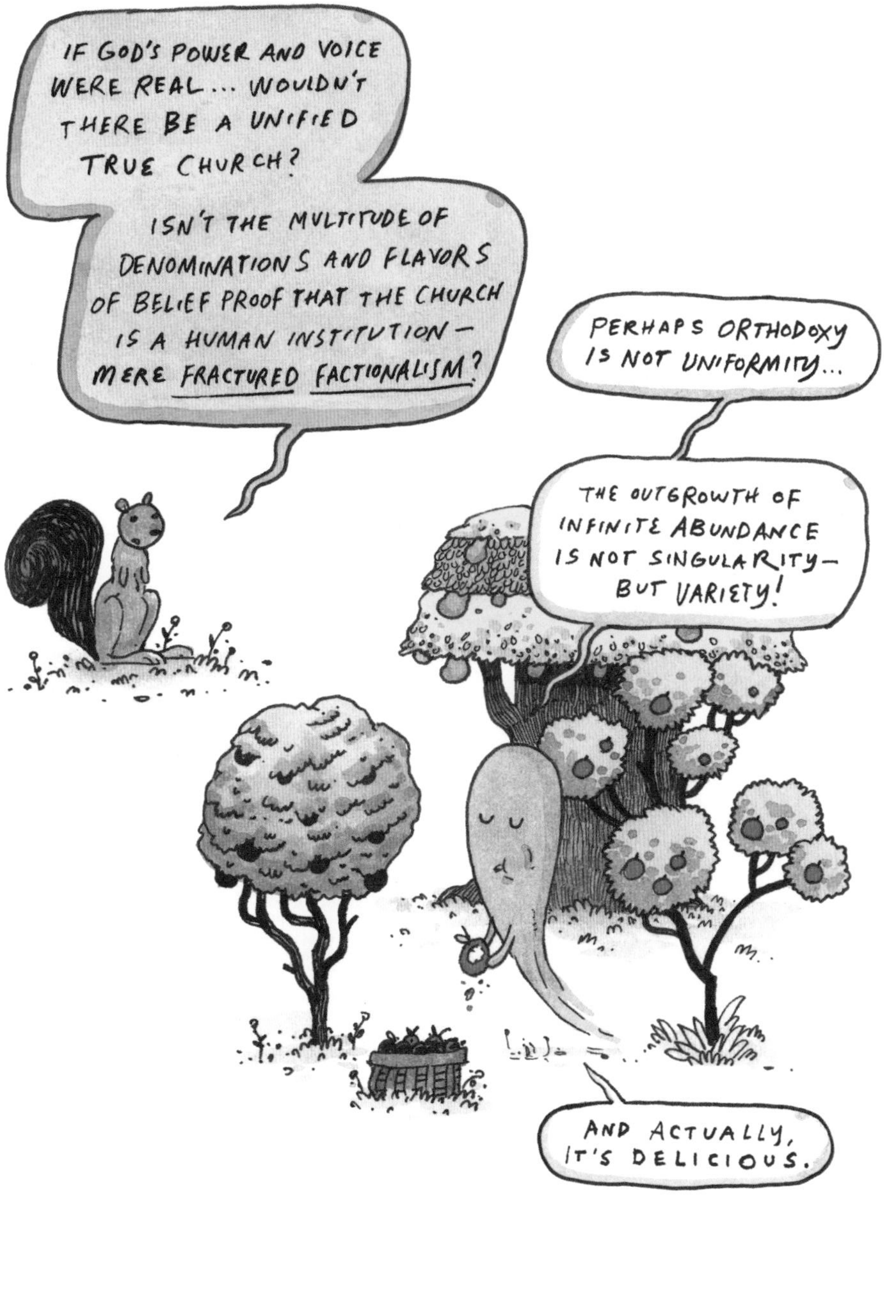
IF GOD'S POWER AND VOICE WERE REAL... WOULDN'T THERE BE A UNIFIED TRUE CHURCH?
ISN'T THE MULTITUDE OF DENOMINATIONS AND FLAVORS OF BELIEF PROOF THAT THE CHURCH IS A HUMAN INSTITUTION— MERE FRACTURED FACTIONALISM?
PERHAPS ORTHODOXY IS NOT UNIFORMITY...
THE OUTGROWTH OF INFINITE ABUNDANCE IS NOT SINGULARITY— BUT VARIETY!
AND ACTUALLY, IT'S DELICIOUS.

THE HO|Y GHOST

THANKS FOR VISITING SANTA, LITTLE ONE.

NOW, BE A GOOD GIRL...

WHY DO WE DO THIS!?

WE LIE TO OUR CHILDREN ABOUT A MAGICAL FIGURE AT THE NORTH POLE, WHO GRANTS... WISHES!?

IT IS CRUEL... WE INDOCTRINATE KIDS INTO THIS FRADULENT LITURGY OF "BELIEF"

""

AS IF "BELIEF" IS THE HIGHEST OF VIRTUES.

EVEN WORSE, IT IS COMPLETE FICTION!

MERRY CHRISTMAS!

BYE SANNA!

IT IS NOT "COMPLETE FICTION."

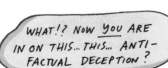

WHAT!? NOW YOU ARE IN ON THIS... THIS... ANTI-FACTUAL DECEPTION?

TRUTH AND FACT ARE VERY SEPARATE VALUES IN GOD'S ECONOMY.

HEY. WAIT. CAN I HAVE A CANDY CANE?

THE ADVENTURES OF THE
HOLY GHOST
THE UNIVERSE IS A MONSTER...
AN ENGINE RUNNING ON CHANCE AND DEATH...
IT'S SO BEAUTIFUL.

THE HOLY GHOST
FART
UH. SORRY.
WHY DID GOD MAKE FARTS? SERIOUSLY.
FUNNY YOU SHOULD ASK. THEY ARE TO REMIND US OF OUR NATURAL INTERNAL CORRUPTION. SEE, YOU CAN NEVER ESCAPE YOUR OWN INNER STATE OF DECAY AND FOUL DEPRAVITY.
...
REALLY?
NAH. THE SOUND JUST MAKES HIM LAUGH.

THE HOLYGHOST

...AND I KNOW
HE WATCHES
OVER ME...

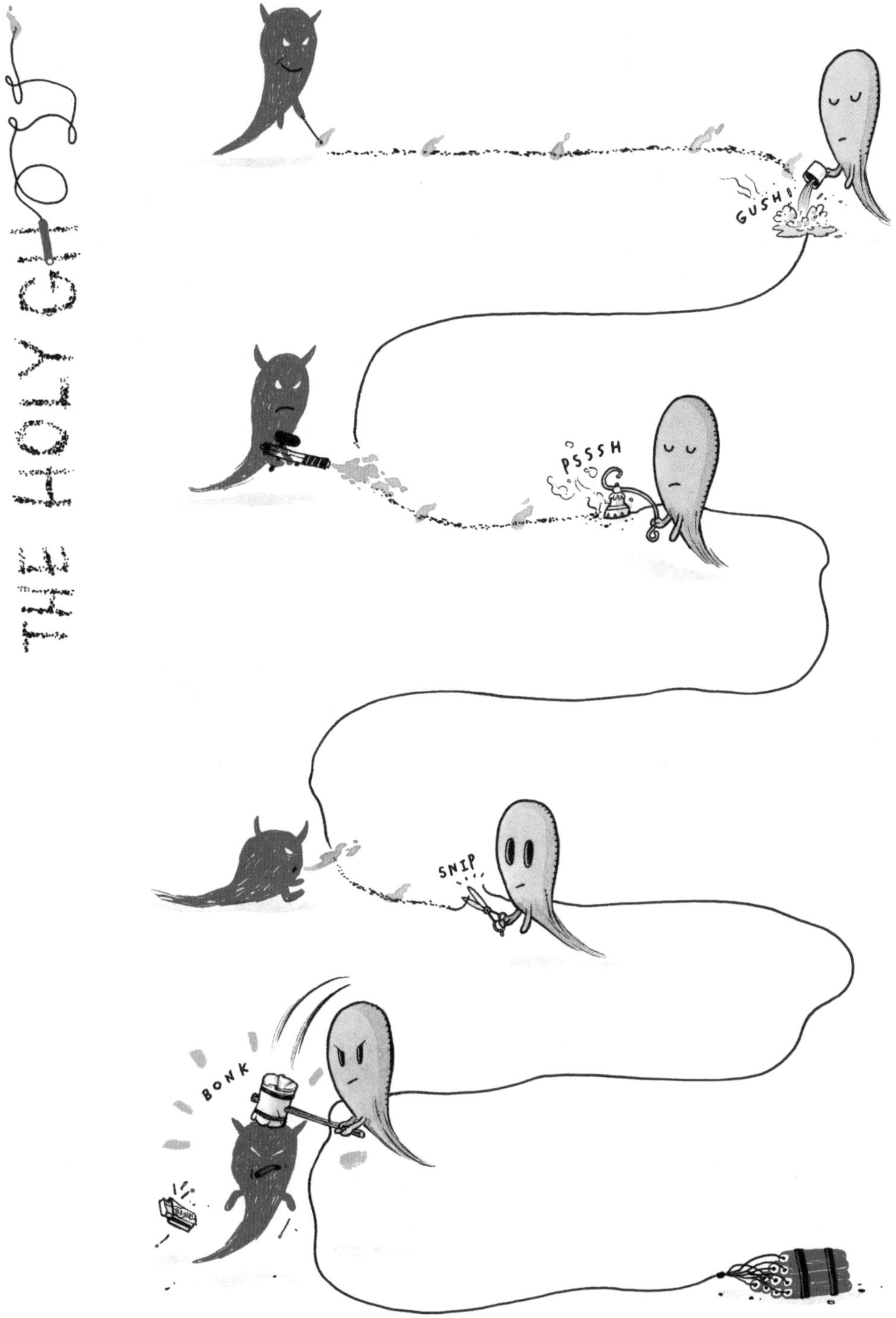
THE HOLY GHOST
GUSH!
PSSSH
SNIP
BONK

THE HOLY GHOST

OH PLEASE, HOLY GOD—PLEASE PLEASE DON'T LET IT BE CANCER... OH PLEASE-PLEASE-PLEASE...
-UGH-
IT'S JUST A PIMPLE.
OH! OK-THANK GOD! OH MAN... PHEW-WELL, ALL RIGHT. OK. SEE YA!
BYE!

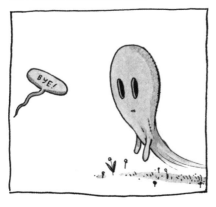

THE HOLY GHOST

SIGH

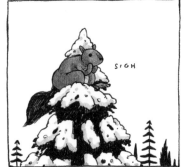

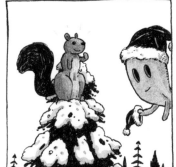

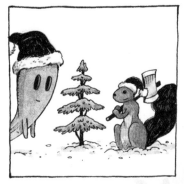

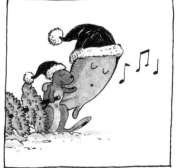

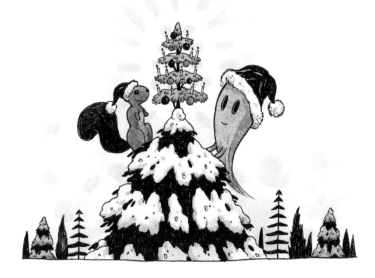

THE HOLY GHOST

I'M... I'M AFRAID.
THERE WILL NEVER BE ANOTHER YOU...
YOU ARE...
A UNIQUE EXPRESSION OF THE COSMOS.
SINGULARITY IS SIGNIFICANCE.
NO—I'M AFRAID OF HEIGHTS.

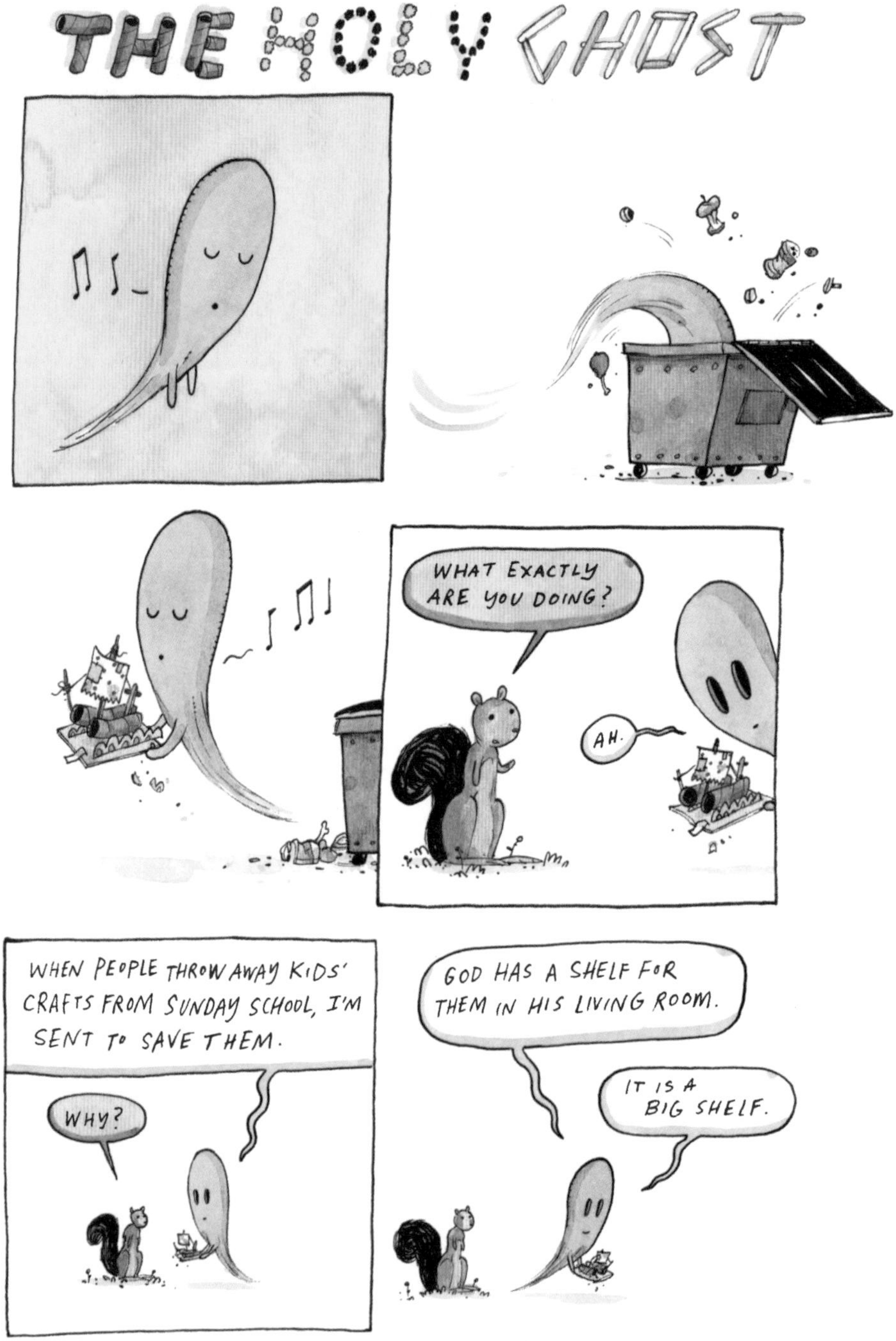
THE HOLY GHOST
WHAT EXACTLY ARE YOU DOING?
AH.
WHEN PEOPLE THROW AWAY KIDS' CRAFTS FROM SUNDAY SCHOOL, I'M SENT TO SAVE THEM.
WHY?
GOD HAS A SHELF FOR THEM IN HIS LIVING ROOM.
IT IS A BIG SHELF.

THE HOLY GHOST

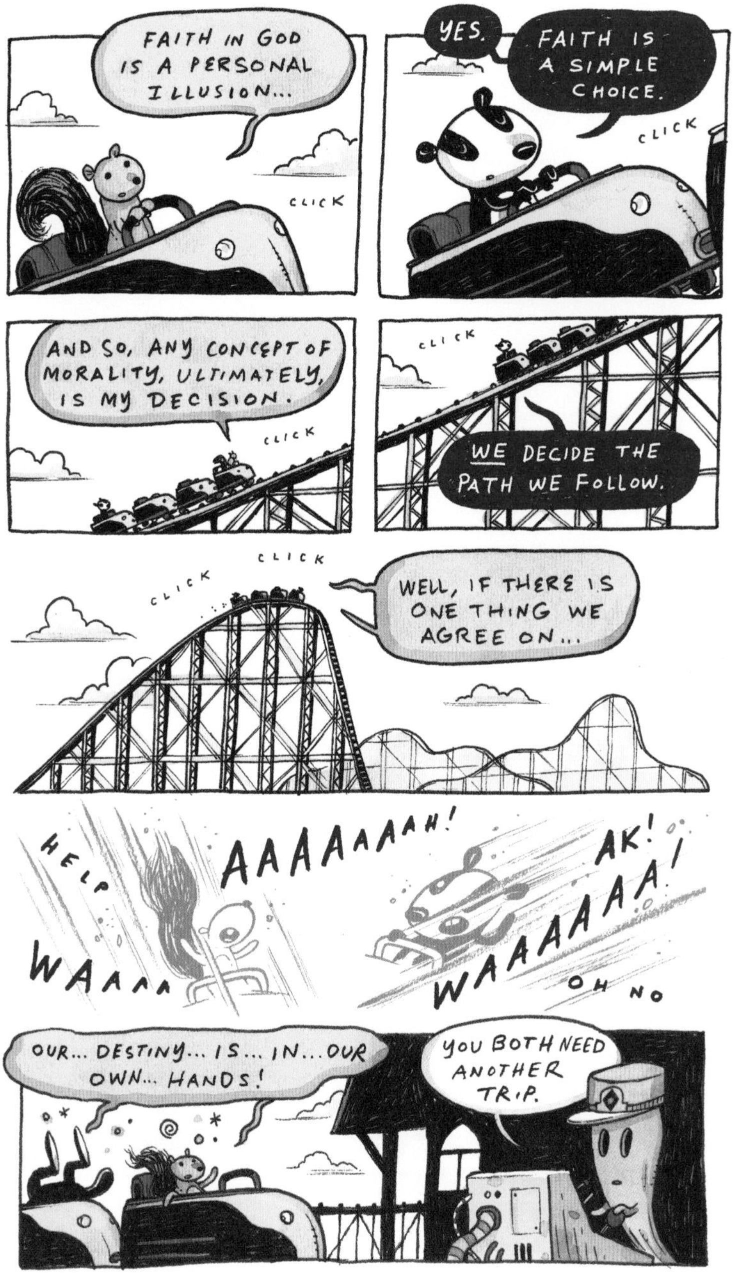
FAITH IN GOD IS A PERSONAL ILLUSION...
CLICK
YES.
FAITH IS A SIMPLE CHOICE.
CLICK
AND SO, ANY CONCEPT OF MORALITY, ULTIMATELY, IS MY DECISION.
CLICK
CLICK
WE DECIDE THE PATH WE FOLLOW.
CLICK
CLICK
WELL, IF THERE IS ONE THING WE AGREE ON...
HELP
AAAAAAAH!
WAAAA
AK!
WAAAAAA!
OH NO
OUR... DESTINY... IS... IN... OUR OWN... HANDS!
YOU BOTH NEED ANOTHER TRIP.

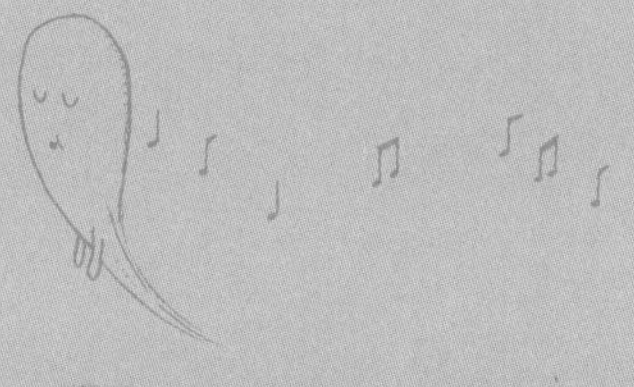

THE HOLY GHOST

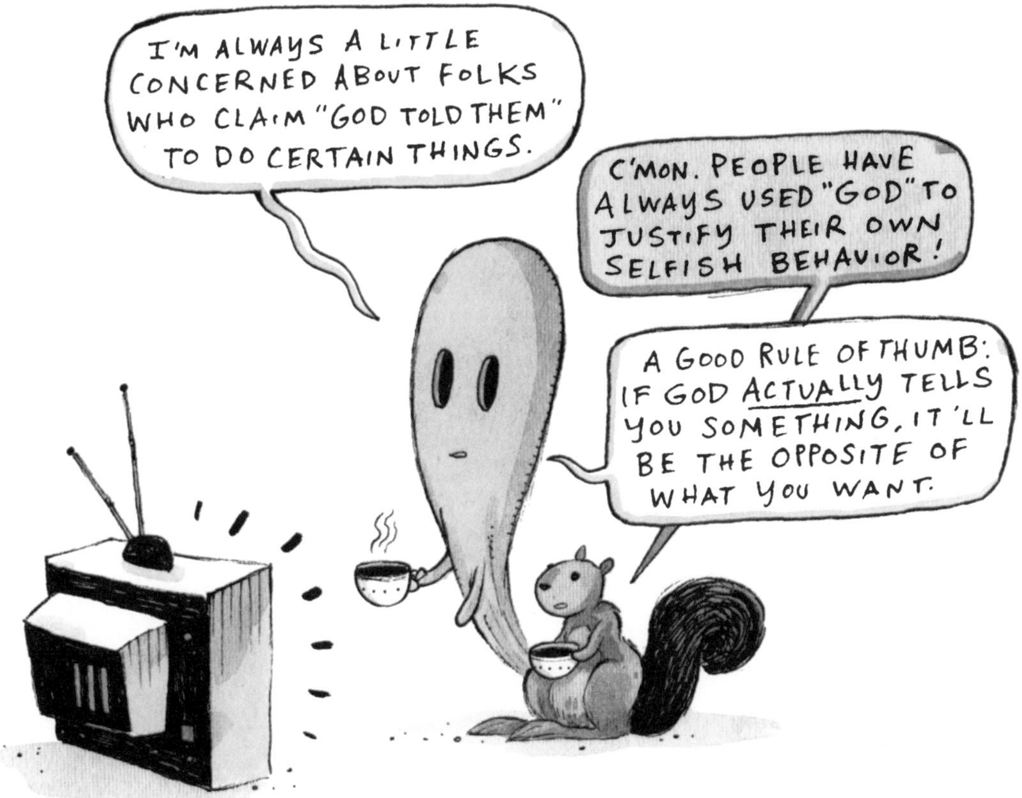
I'M ALWAYS A LITTLE CONCERNED ABOUT FOLKS WHO CLAIM "GOD TOLD THEM" TO DO CERTAIN THINGS.
C'MON. PEOPLE HAVE ALWAYS USED "GOD" TO JUSTIFY THEIR OWN SELFISH BEHAVIOR!
A GOOD RULE OF THUMB: IF GOD ACTUALLY TELLS YOU SOMETHING, IT'LL BE THE OPPOSITE OF WHAT YOU WANT.

THE HOLY GHOST

I'M SURPRISED YOU LIKE HALLOWEEN.
WHAT'S NOT TO LIKE?
NEIGHBORS BEING KIND TO CHILDREN, COMMUNITIES GETTING TO KNOW EACH OTHER BY GIVING AWAY GIFTS TO TOTAL STRANGERS!
OH, WELL, I JUST ASSUMED THAT IT WAS YOU-KNOW-WHO'S BIG DAY...
WHO, SATAN? NAH. HE HATES HALLOWEEN.
HE DOES HIS BEST WORK DURING CHRISTMAS.

THE HOLY GHOST

WHY WOULD GOD NOT MAKE US ALL, LIKE, SUPER?
SURE, WE ALL WANT THE POWERS. BUT EVEN MORE, WE WANT TO BE INDESTRUCTABLE!
BUT INSTEAD OF STEEL, WE ARE A FLESHY BAG OF GOO! WOUNDED EVEN BY THE EDGE OF A SHEET OF PAPER.
THERE MUST BE SOMETHING IMPORTANT TO GOD ABOUT...
FRAGILITY.

the holy ghost

UGH! THESE... WEEDS...
YOU KNOW, YOU ARE ALSO PULLING UP THE FLOWERS.
RIP
RIP
GAH! IT'S HOPELESS!
I'LL NEVER GET ALL OF THEM— IF I DO, THEY'LL JUST GROW BACK!
WELL, ISN'T BASIC UNHAPPINESS A NATURAL RESPONSE TO A DIFFICULT AND IMPERFECT UNIVERSE?
TECHNICALLY, YOU CAN'T BE HOPELESS. SEE, WITHOUT DISCONTENT THERE CAN BE NO HOPE AT ALL.
WORST. PEP TALK. EVER.

THE HOLY GHOST

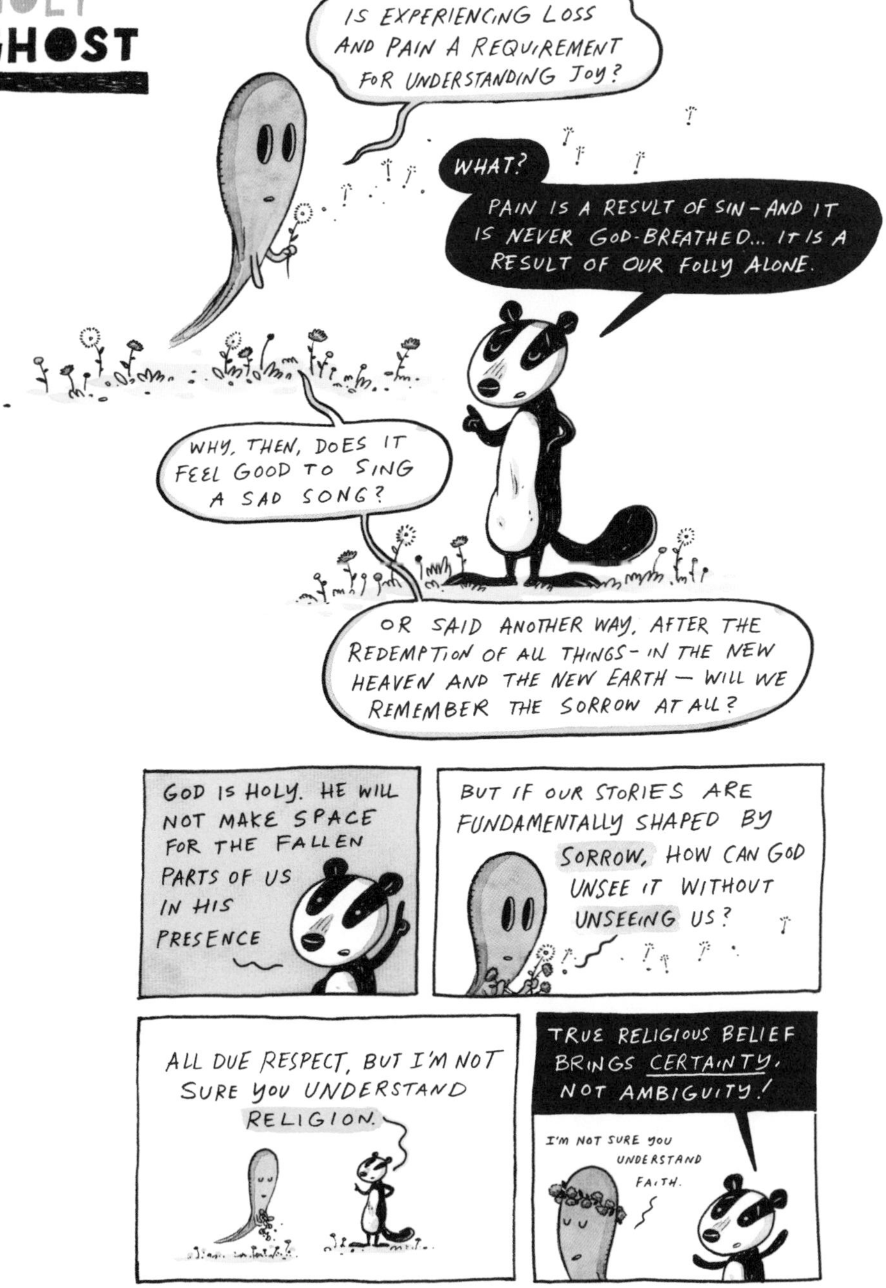
IS EXPERIENCING LOSS AND PAIN A REQUIREMENT FOR UNDERSTANDING JOY?
WHAT?
PAIN IS A RESULT OF SIN—AND IT IS NEVER GOD-BREATHED... IT IS A RESULT OF OUR FOLLY ALONE.
WHY, THEN, DOES IT FEEL GOOD TO SING A SAD SONG?
OR SAID ANOTHER WAY, AFTER THE REDEMPTION OF ALL THINGS—IN THE NEW HEAVEN AND THE NEW EARTH—WILL WE REMEMBER THE SORROW AT ALL?
GOD IS HOLY. HE WILL NOT MAKE SPACE FOR THE FALLEN PARTS OF US IN HIS PRESENCE
BUT IF OUR STORIES ARE FUNDAMENTALLY SHAPED BY SORROW, HOW CAN GOD UNSEE IT WITHOUT UNSEEING US?
ALL DUE RESPECT, BUT I'M NOT SURE YOU UNDERSTAND RELIGION.
TRUE RELIGIOUS BELIEF BRINGS CERTAINTY, NOT AMBIGUITY!
I'M NOT SURE YOU UNDERSTAND FAITH.

THE HOLY GHOST

POOF
POOF
WHOA. WHAT IS THAT?
A MURMURATION. A SINGLE EXPRESSION OF A MASS CONSCIOUSNESS.
DON'T YOU THINK YOU HAVE ENOUGH?
POOF
POOF
PERHAPS GOD'S VAST CREATIVE MIND CAN ONLY BE EXPRESSED IN OUR WORLD BY ENDLESS REPETITION...
SEEMS EXCESSIVE.
POOF
THAT ONE WOULD DISAGREE.

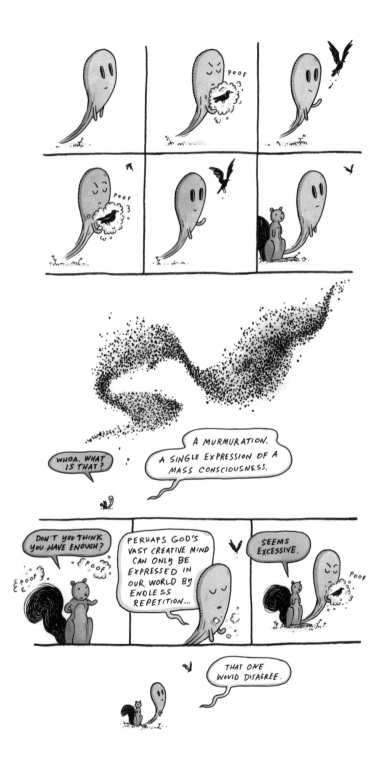

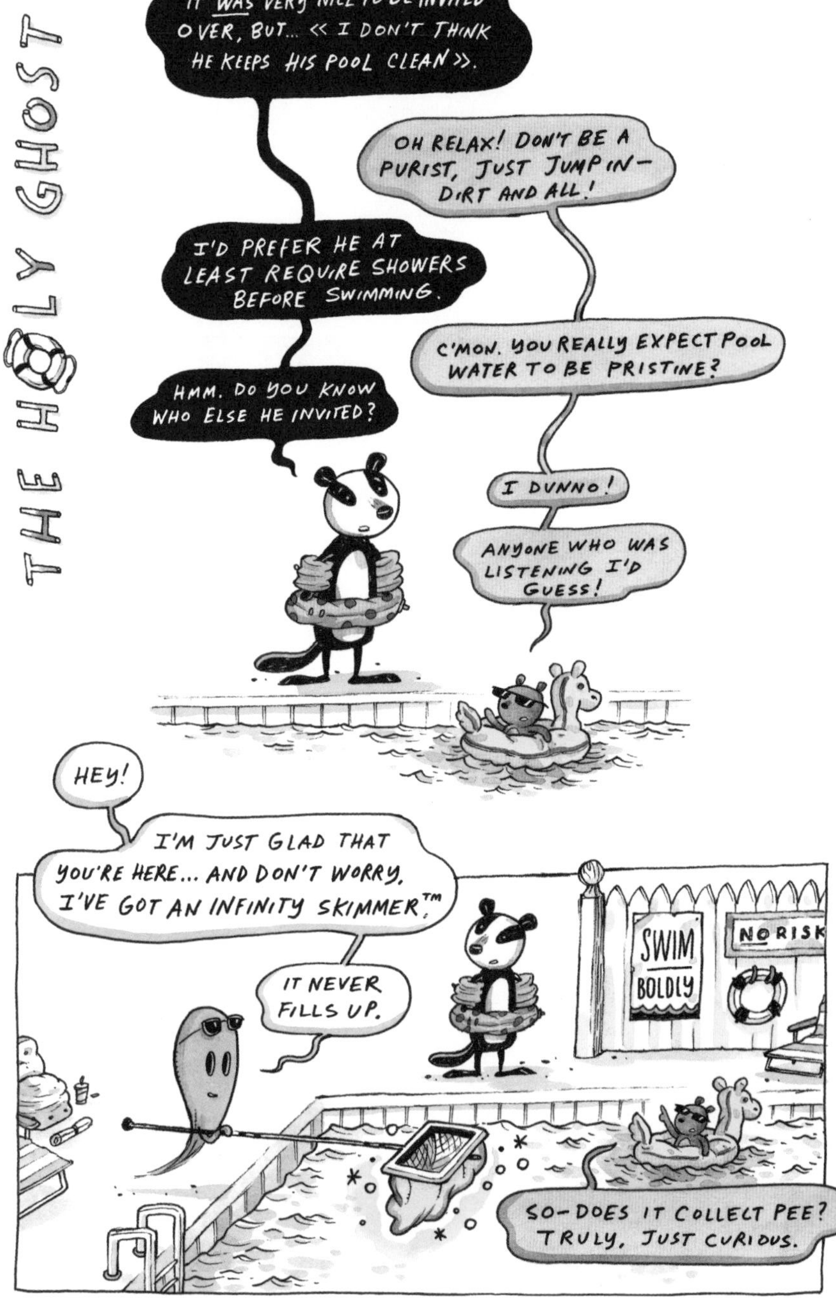
THE HOLY GHOST
IT WAS VERY NICE TO BE INVITED OVER, BUT... « I DON'T THINK HE KEEPS HIS POOL CLEAN ».
OH RELAX! DON'T BE A PURIST, JUST JUMP IN— DIRT AND ALL!
I'D PREFER HE AT LEAST REQUIRE SHOWERS BEFORE SWIMMING.
C'MON. YOU REALLY EXPECT POOL WATER TO BE PRISTINE?
HMM. DO YOU KNOW WHO ELSE HE INVITED?
I DUNNO!
ANYONE WHO WAS LISTENING I'D GUESS!
HEY!
I'M JUST GLAD THAT YOU'RE HERE... AND DON'T WORRY, I'VE GOT AN INFINITY SKIMMER™.
IT NEVER FILLS UP.
SWIM BOLDLY
NO RISK
SO—DOES IT COLLECT PEE? TRULY, JUST CURIOUS.

THE HOLY GHOST

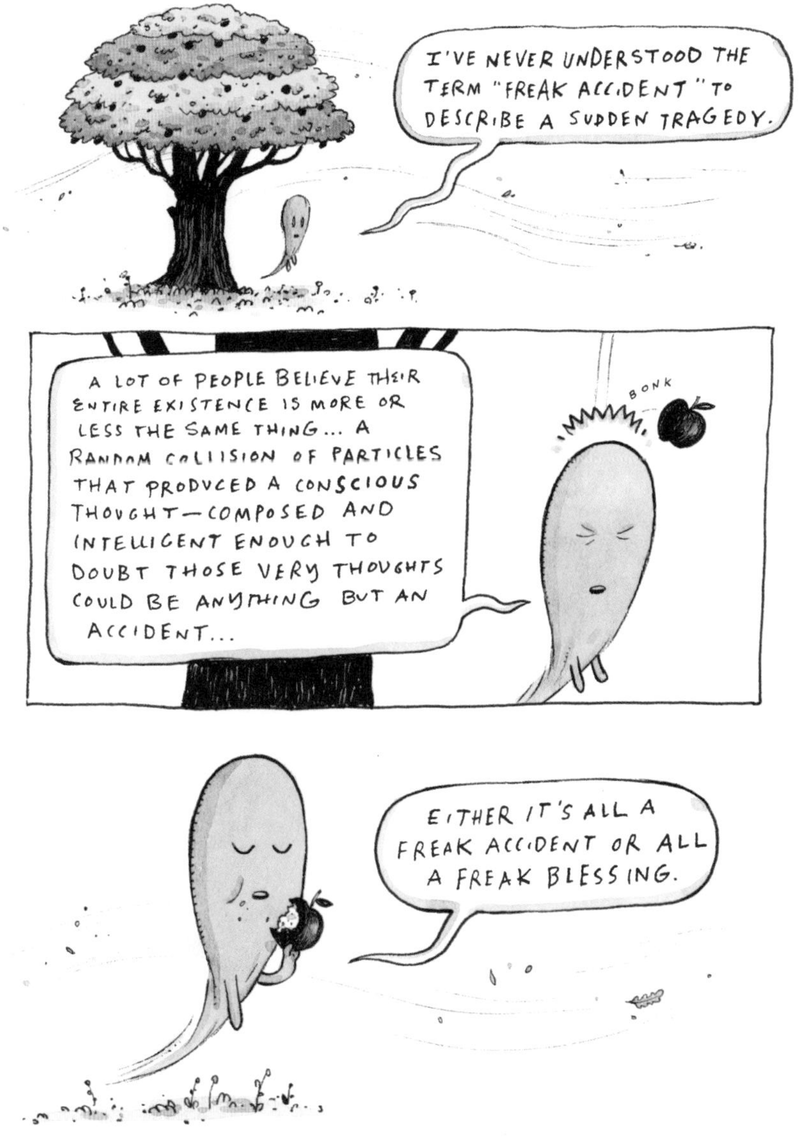
I'VE NEVER UNDERSTOOD THE TERM "FREAK ACCIDENT" TO DESCRIBE A SUDDEN TRAGEDY.
A LOT OF PEOPLE BELIEVE THEIR ENTIRE EXISTENCE IS MORE OR LESS THE SAME THING... A RANDOM COLLISION OF PARTICLES THAT PRODUCED A CONSCIOUS THOUGHT—COMPOSED AND INTELLIGENT ENOUGH TO DOUBT THOSE VERY THOUGHTS COULD BE ANYTHING BUT AN ACCIDENT...
BONK
EITHER IT'S ALL A FREAK ACCIDENT OR ALL A FREAK BLESSING.

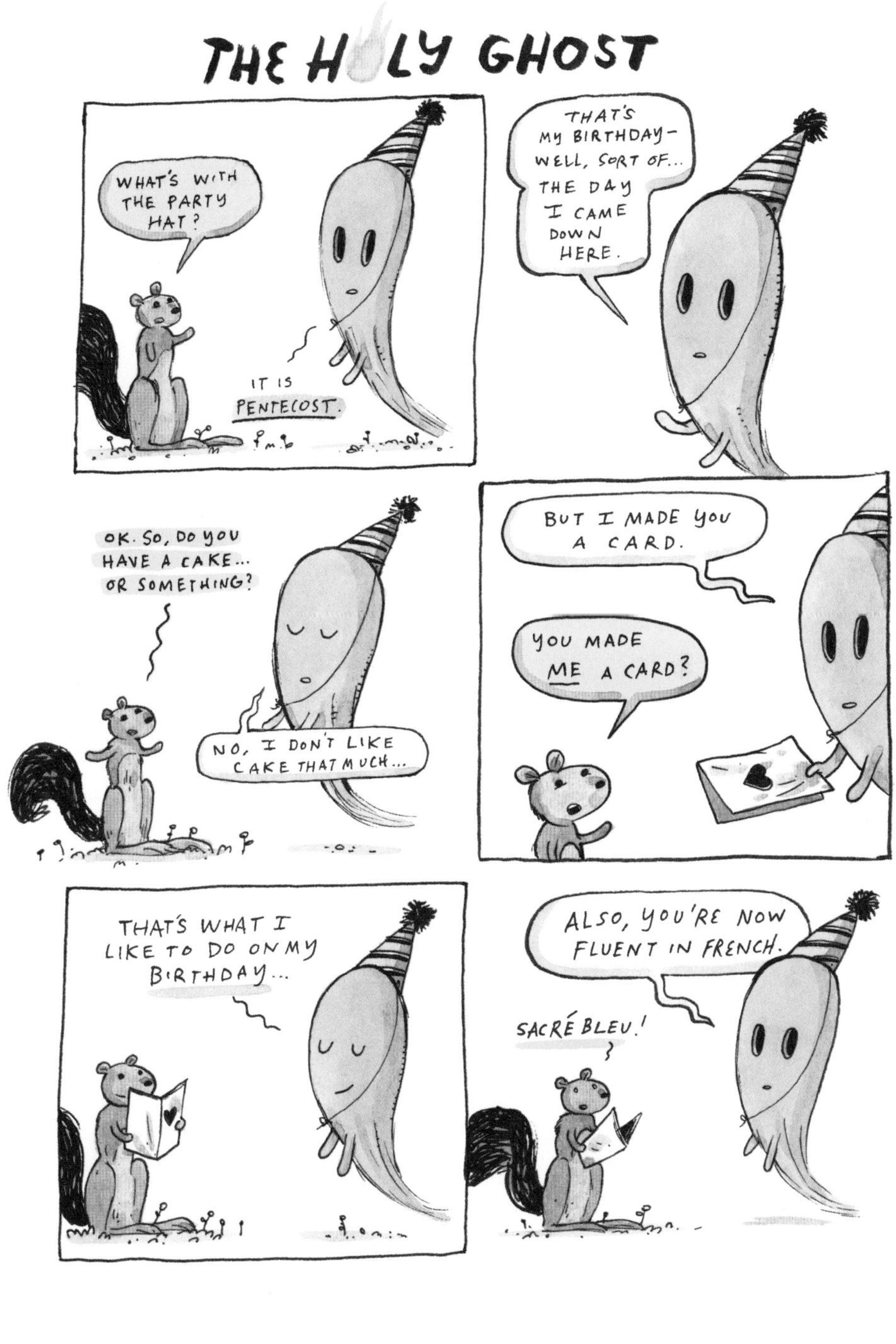
THE HOLY GHOST
WHAT'S WITH THE PARTY HAT?
IT IS PENTECOST.
THAT'S MY BIRTHDAY— WELL, SORT OF... THE DAY I CAME DOWN HERE.
OK. SO, DO YOU HAVE A CAKE... OR SOMETHING?
NO, I DON'T LIKE CAKE THAT MUCH...
BUT I MADE YOU A CARD.
YOU MADE ME A CARD?
THAT'S WHAT I LIKE TO DO ON MY BIRTHDAY...
ALSO, YOU'RE NOW FLUENT IN FRENCH.
SACRÉ BLEU!

THE HOLY GHOST

UGH. WHY WOULD GOD MAKE A BROKEN WORLD WITH ALL THIS EVIL?
UGH. WHY WOULD GOD MAKE A BROKEN WORLD WITH ALL THIS BEAUTY?

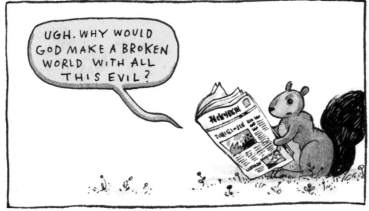

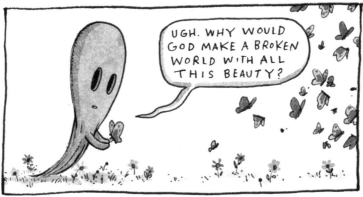

THE HOLY GHOST

BELIEF IN GOD IS BINARY: YES OR NO. SO, I DON'T GET ALL THE DIFFERENT RELIGIONS! AT THE CORE THEY'RE ALL THE SAME, RIGHT? DOGMA SEEMS LIKE EXCLUSIONARY POWER-GRABS.

THEY ALL COME FROM A FEW CRITICAL QUESTIONS... NOT ABOUT DOGMA, BUT ABOUT GOD'S INTENTIONS.

HERE, I MADE YOU A CHART.

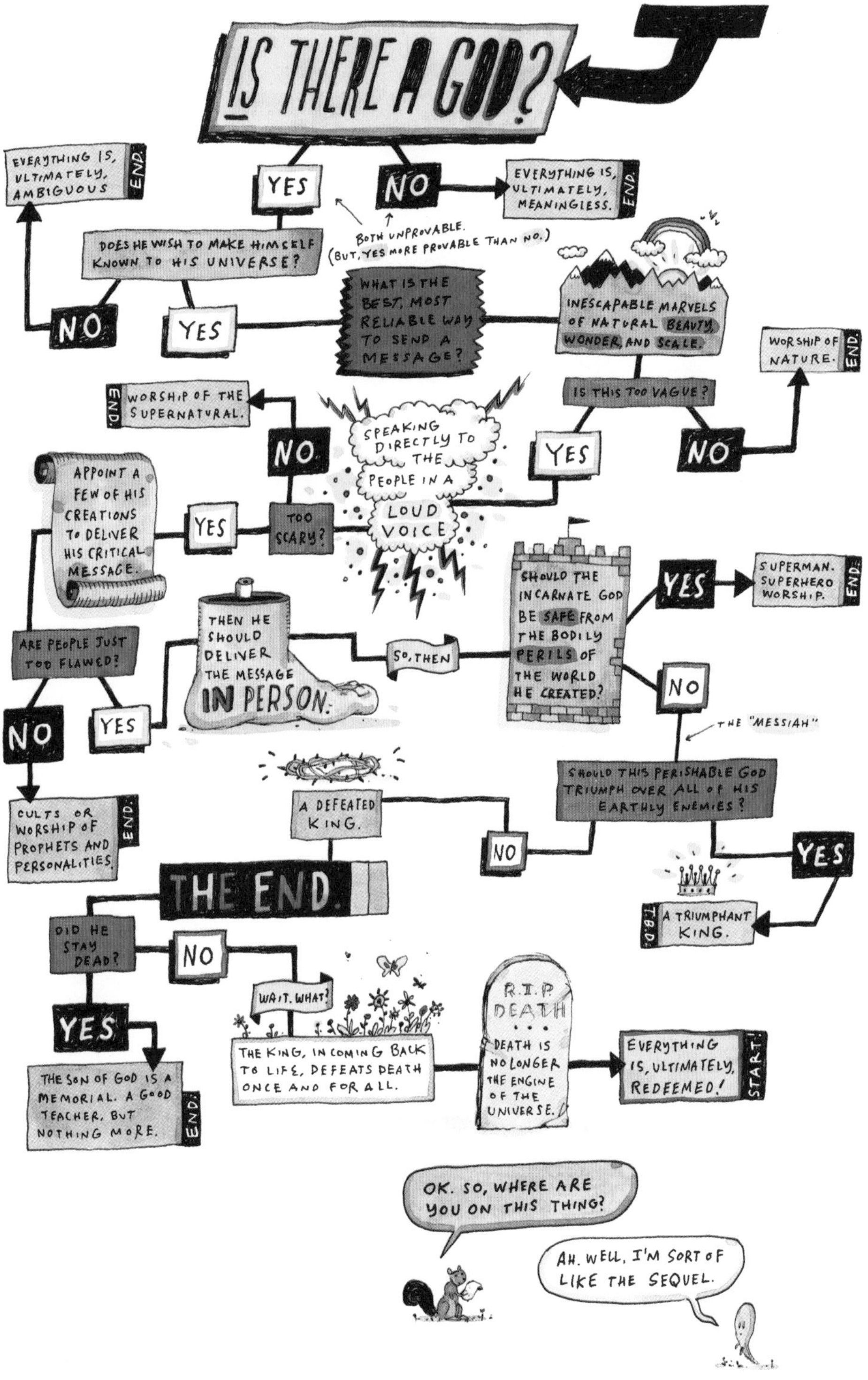
IS THERE A GOD?
YES
NO
EVERYTHING IS, ULTIMATELY, MEANINGLESS. END.
EVERYTHING IS, ULTIMATELY, AMBIGUOUS END.
BOTH UNPROVABLE. (BUT, YES MORE PROVABLE THAN NO.)
DOES HE WISH TO MAKE HIMSELF KNOWN TO HIS UNIVERSE?
NO
YES
WHAT IS THE BEST, MOST RELIABLE WAY TO SEND A MESSAGE?
INESCAPABLE MARVELS OF NATURAL BEAUTY, WONDER, AND SCALE.
IS THIS TOO VAGUE?
NO
WORSHIP OF NATURE. END.
YES
SPEAKING DIRECTLY TO THE PEOPLE IN A LOUD VOICE
TOO SCARY?
NO
END. WORSHIP OF THE SUPERNATURAL.
YES
APPOINT A FEW OF HIS CREATIONS TO DELIVER HIS CRITICAL MESSAGE.
ARE PEOPLE JUST TOO FLAWED?
NO
CULTS OR WORSHIP OF PROPHETS AND PERSONALITIES. END.
YES
THEN HE SHOULD DELIVER THE MESSAGE IN PERSON.
SO, THEN
SHOULD THE INCARNATE GOD BE SAFE FROM THE BODILY PERILS OF THE WORLD HE CREATED?
YES
SUPERMAN. SUPERHERO WORSHIP. END.
NO
THE "MESSIAH"
SHOULD THIS PERISHABLE GOD TRIUMPH OVER ALL OF HIS EARTHLY ENEMIES?
YES
T.B.D. A TRIUMPHANT KING.
NO
A DEFEATED KING.
THE END.
DID HE STAY DEAD?
YES
THE SON OF GOD IS A MEMORIAL. A GOOD TEACHER, BUT NOTHING MORE. END.
NO
WAIT. WHAT?
THE KING, IN COMING BACK TO LIFE, DEFEATS DEATH ONCE AND FOR ALL.
R.I.P. DEATH
DEATH IS NO LONGER THE ENGINE OF THE UNIVERSE.
EVERYTHING IS, ULTIMATELY, REDEEMED! START.
OK. SO, WHERE ARE YOU ON THIS THING?
AH. WELL, I'M SORT OF LIKE THE SEQUEL.

THE HOLY GHOST

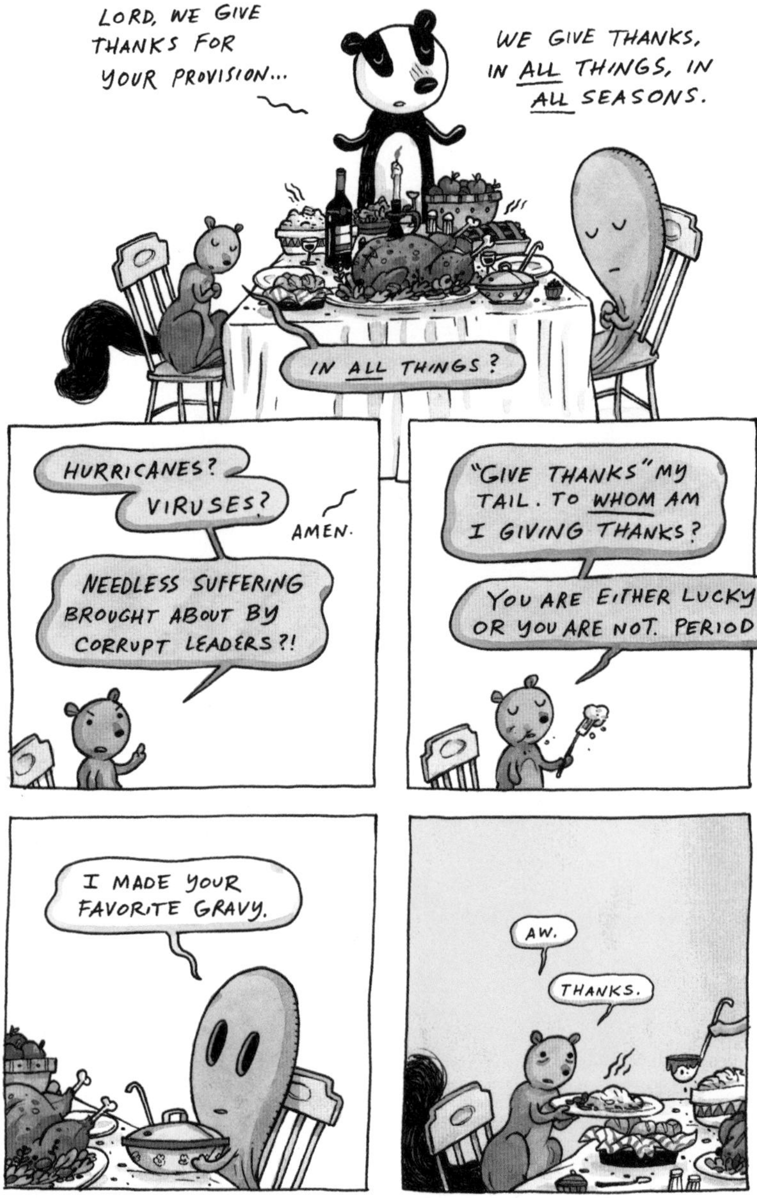
LORD, WE GIVE THANKS FOR YOUR PROVISION...
WE GIVE THANKS, IN ALL THINGS, IN ALL SEASONS.
IN ALL THINGS?
HURRICANES? VIRUSES?
AMEN.
NEEDLESS SUFFERING BROUGHT ABOUT BY CORRUPT LEADERS?!
"GIVE THANKS" MY TAIL. TO WHOM AM I GIVING THANKS?
YOU ARE EITHER LUCKY OR YOU ARE NOT. PERIOD.
I MADE YOUR FAVORITE GRAVY.
AW.
THANKS.

THE HOLY GHOST

NOEL...
NOEL...
NOEL...
PEEK
BORN IS THE KING OF ISRAEL!

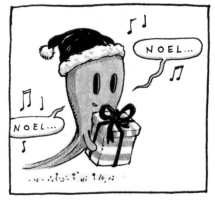

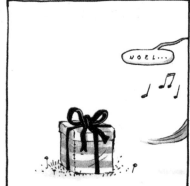

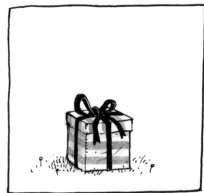

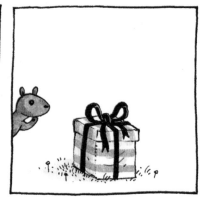

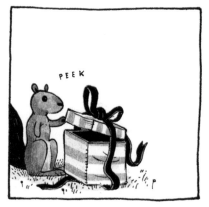

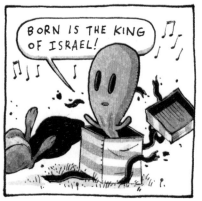

THE HOLY GHOST

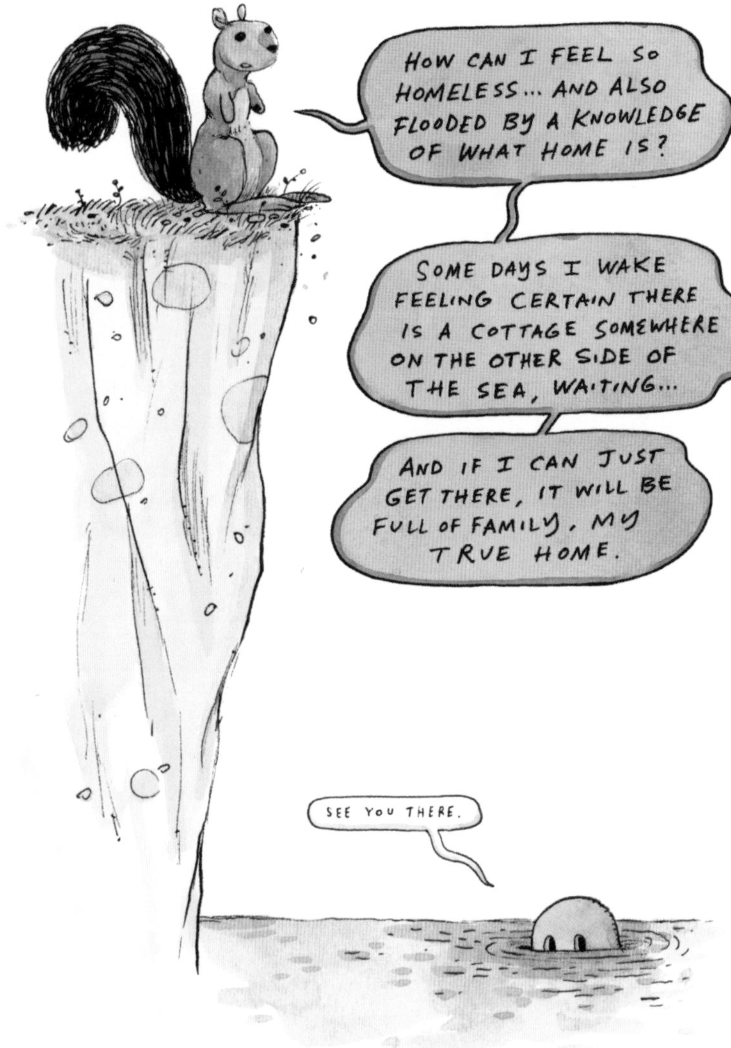
HOW CAN I FEEL SO HOMELESS... AND ALSO FLOODED BY A KNOWLEDGE OF WHAT HOME IS?
SOME DAYS I WAKE FEELING CERTAIN THERE IS A COTTAGE SOMEWHERE ON THE OTHER SIDE OF THE SEA, WAITING...
AND IF I CAN JUST GET THERE, IT WILL BE FULL OF FAMILY, MY TRUE HOME.
SEE YOU THERE.

THE HLY GHOST

BILLIONS OF YEARS IN THE MAKING, THE GRAVITATIONAL COLLAPSE OF A MASSIVE STAR EMITS A STELLAR EXPLOSION, CALLED A SUPERNOVA, THAT BRIEFLY OUTSHINES THE LIGHT OF THE ENTIRE GALAXY, EQUAL TO THE ENERGY THE STAR EMITTED OVER ITS LIFE SPAN.

NO SINGLE PERSON COULD EVER MATCH THE RANDOM AND CRUEL DESTRUCTIVE POWER OF AN AVERAGE SUPERNOVA.

IS THE UNIVERSE EVIL, OR IS IT JUST NATURE?

THAT'S RIDICULOUS. A STAR CAN'T BE EVIL...

SO, IF EVIL IS NOT PART OF THE NATURAL UNIVERSE... AND WE ARE PRODUCTS OF THAT VERY UNIVERSE...

THEN WHERE DOES EVIL COME FROM?

DID YOU BRING THE BUG SPRAY?

The Holy Ghost

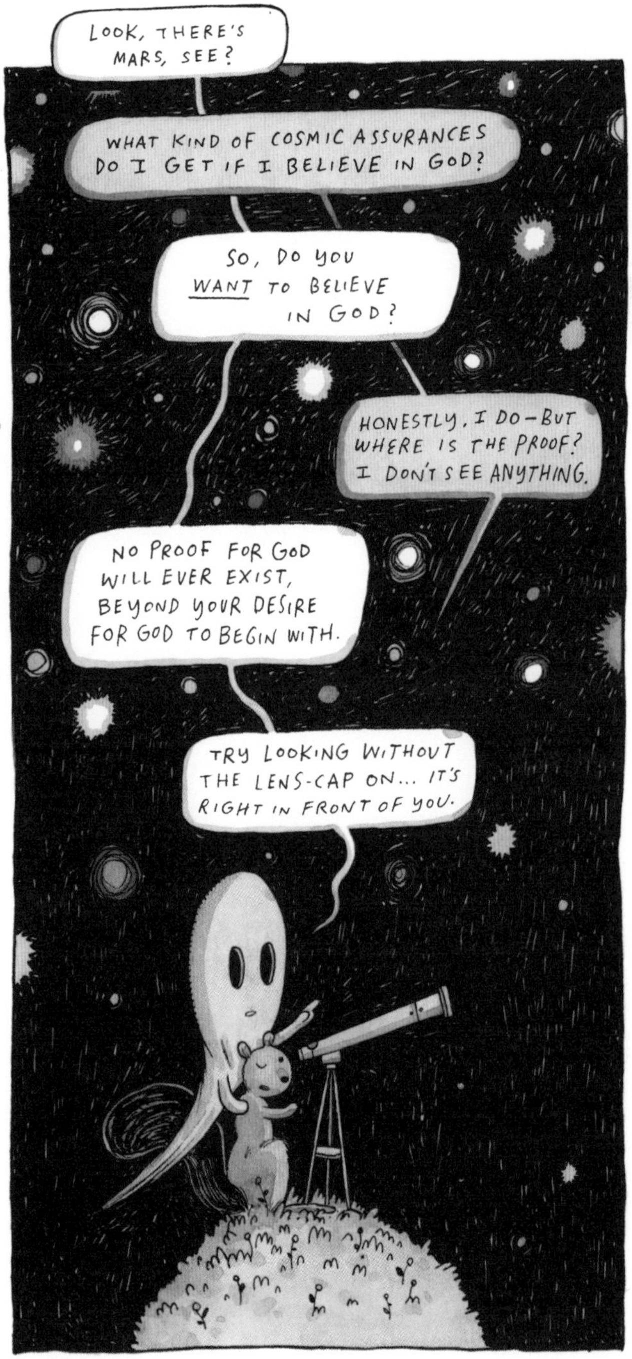

THE HOLY GHOST

LOVE...
IS EASY-
WHEN WE CHOOSE TO LOVE
ONLY THE LOVABLE.

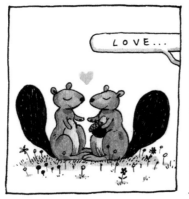

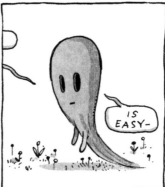

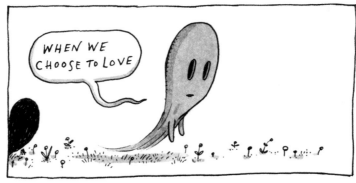

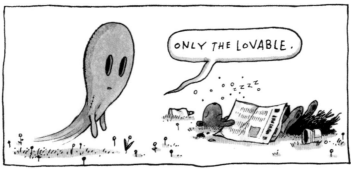

THE HOLY GHOST

I'M GLAD YOU LOVE DOLLY BUT REMEMBER, DON'T LOVE HER TOO MUCH, MORE THAN GOD, OR HE WILL COME AND TAKE HER AWAY.
<SNIFF>
<SNIFF>
<SNIFF>
<POP>
OH, NOT TO WORRY SWEETHEART... ADULTS ARE TOO OLD TO REMEMBER I LIVE IN HERE.

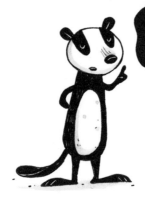

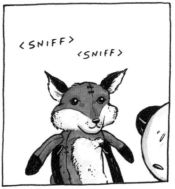

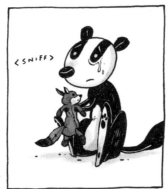

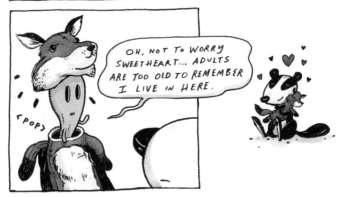

THE HOLY GHOST

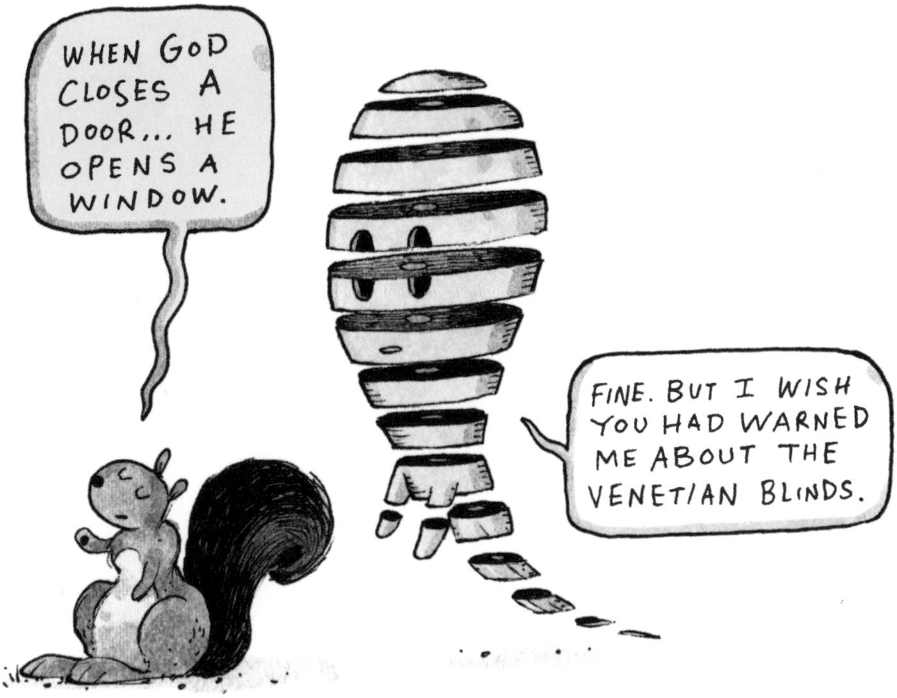
WHEN GOD CLOSES A DOOR... HE OPENS A WINDOW.
FINE. BUT I WISH YOU HAD WARNED ME ABOUT THE VENETIAN BLINDS.

the HOLY GHOST

LET ME SEE YOUR TAIL A SECOND...

UH...

WHOA! WHAT ARE YOU DOING?

POP

JUST REPLACING YOUR ANTENNA.

WHAT!?

EVERYONE HAS AN ANTENNA DESIGNED JUST FOR YOU BY GOD HIMSELF...

NO WAY.

WELL, GOD TALKS TO PEOPLE IN MANY DIFFERENT WAYS, DEPENDING ON THE KIND OF ANTENNA THAT FITS BEST.

CAN I SEE!?

OK, HERE'S YOUR STANDARD "FACES OF CHILDREN"... THEN "BEAUTIFUL SUNSET" WITH A VERY EFFECTIVE NOSTALGIA UPGRADE...

HERE'S THE OFTEN-REQUESTED "PROPHETIC DREAMS & VISIONS" BUT NOBODY GETS THESE ANYMORE... MOSTLY...

HOLD ON! WHAT DID I JUST GET?

UH...

WELL. YOU GOT "PAIN AND PERSONAL FAILURE." THEY AREN'T VERY POPULAR, BUT THEY WORK THE BEST.

GREAT.

THE HOLY GHOST

OH, SPIRIT...
REVEAL TO ME THE SINNERS...
THE WRETCHED AND BROKEN—
THE FOULEST, IN MOST DESPERATE NEED OF YOU.

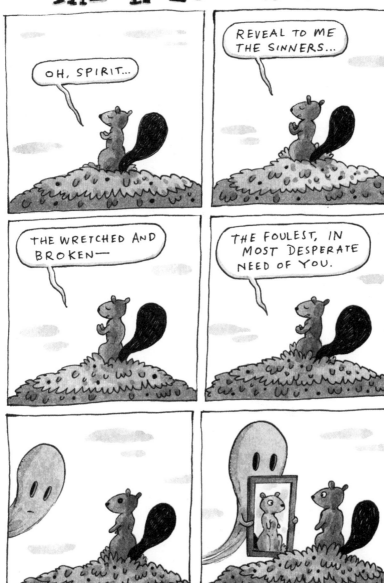

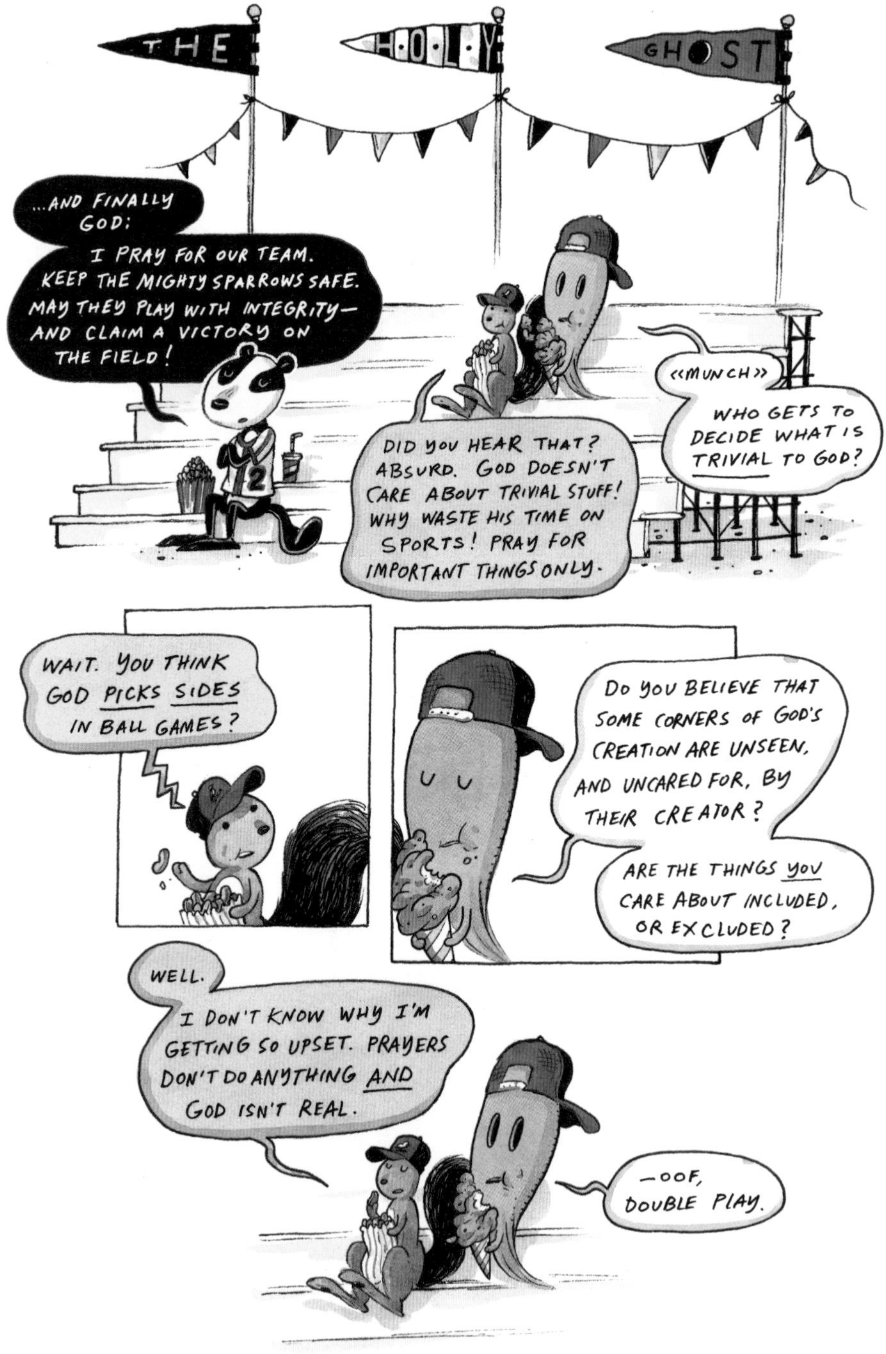
THE HOLY GHOST
...AND FINALLY GOD: I PRAY FOR OUR TEAM. KEEP THE MIGHTY SPARROWS SAFE. MAY THEY PLAY WITH INTEGRITY— AND CLAIM A VICTORY ON THE FIELD!
DID YOU HEAR THAT? ABSURD. GOD DOESN'T CARE ABOUT TRIVIAL STUFF! WHY WASTE HIS TIME ON SPORTS! PRAY FOR IMPORTANT THINGS ONLY.
«MUNCH» WHO GETS TO DECIDE WHAT IS TRIVIAL TO GOD?
WAIT. YOU THINK GOD PICKS SIDES IN BALL GAMES?
DO YOU BELIEVE THAT SOME CORNERS OF GOD'S CREATION ARE UNSEEN, AND UNCARED FOR, BY THEIR CREATOR?
ARE THE THINGS YOU CARE ABOUT INCLUDED, OR EXCLUDED?
WELL. I DON'T KNOW WHY I'M GETTING SO UPSET. PRAYERS DON'T DO ANYTHING AND GOD ISN'T REAL.
—OOF, DOUBLE PLAY.

THE HOLY GHOST

I DO NOT BELIEVE IN GOD. I BELIEVE IN SCIENCE. A.M.A.
SCIENCE -IS- IDOLATRY. CHANGE MY MIND
HMM.
CAN WE APPLAUD HAMLET... WITHOUT PRAISING SHAKESPEARE?

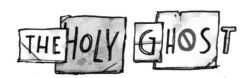

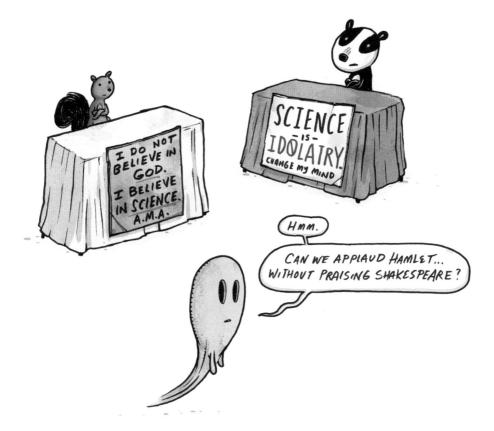

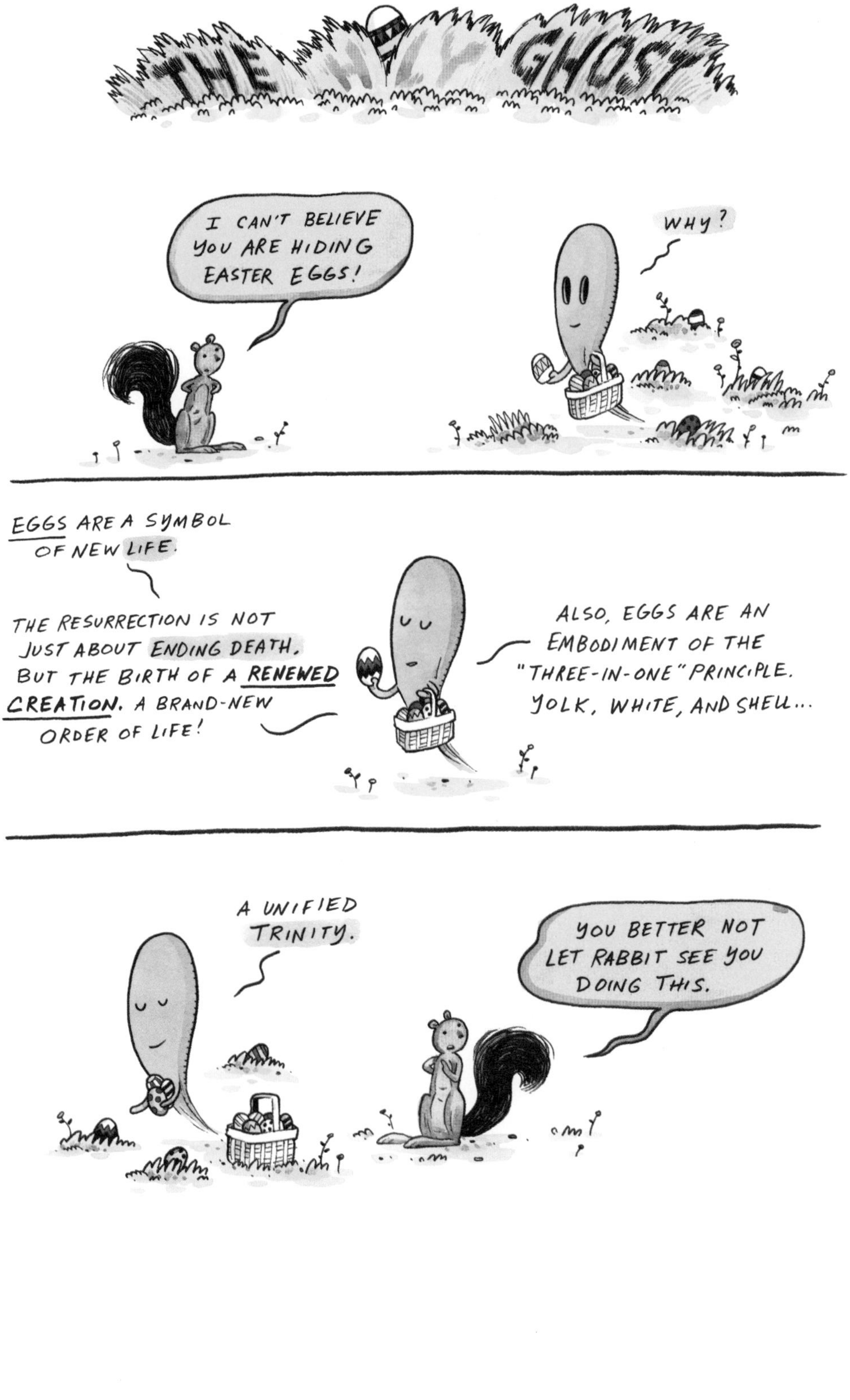
THE HOLY GHOST
I CAN'T BELIEVE YOU ARE HIDING EASTER EGGS!
WHY?
EGGS ARE A SYMBOL OF NEW LIFE.
THE RESURRECTION IS NOT JUST ABOUT ENDING DEATH, BUT THE BIRTH OF A RENEWED CREATION. A BRAND-NEW ORDER OF LIFE!
ALSO, EGGS ARE AN EMBODIMENT OF THE "THREE-IN-ONE" PRINCIPLE. YOLK, WHITE, AND SHELL...
A UNIFIED TRINITY.
YOU BETTER NOT LET RABBIT SEE YOU DOING THIS.

THE HOLY GHOST

RELIGIOUS PEOPLE ARE SO JUDGMENTAL. I JUST FIND THE CONCEPT OF SIN TOTALLY REVOLTING.
SO, YOU DON'T THINK THE WORLD IS FULL OF CORRUPT AND SELFISH BEHAVIOR?
WHAT! ARE YOU KIDDING?
LOOK AROUND—EVIL IS EVERYWHERE! GREEDY POLITICIANS! PRIDEFUL BANKERS! UNJUST POLICE! ANGRY DRIVERS! RUDE STORE CLERKS!
OK, SO, I'M FINE WITH SIN AS LONG AS IT APPLIES TO OTHER PEOPLE...

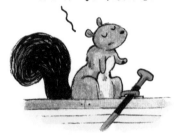

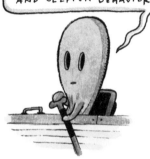

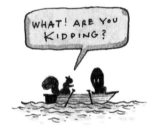

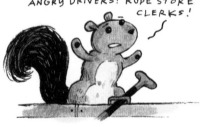

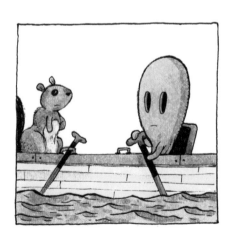

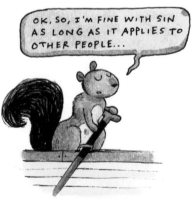

THE HOLY GHOST
DOESN'T THE IDEA OF HEAVEN STRIKE YOU AS ABSURD?
SUPERSTITIOUS PEOPLE ARE SICK OF THEIR HARD LIVES, SO THEY INVENT A MAGICAL FANTASY LAND TO GIVE THEM HOPE...
"PIE-IN-THE SKY"?
EXACTLY. HA. ...YOU KNOW, LIKE, EVERYONE GETS A PONY AND A HUGE MANSION...
...AND EVERYONE'S DEEPEST LONGINGS ARE FINALLY REALIZED?
HA. TOTALLY. LIKE, NO ONE FEARS DEATH'S TAKING WHAT THEY LOVE ANYMORE...
AND, OUR WORK ISN'T TAINTED WITH ENDLESS FUTILITY...
YOU KNOW, A PLACE WHERE THERE ARE NO TEARS. AND... EVERYTHING SAD BECOMES UNTRUE. AND NO PART OF THE WORLD IS TOO SMALL TO BE REDEEMED–REBORN IN NEWNESS AND LIFE...
AND WE BECOME TRULY ALIVE, IN THE LIGHT OF THE REAL SOURCE FOR ALL OUR LONGINGS. A HOME–THE PURPOSE FOR OUR VERY CREATION...
YOU KNOW, SOMETHING, UH, TOTALLY STUPID LIKE THAT.
ANOTHER SLICE?

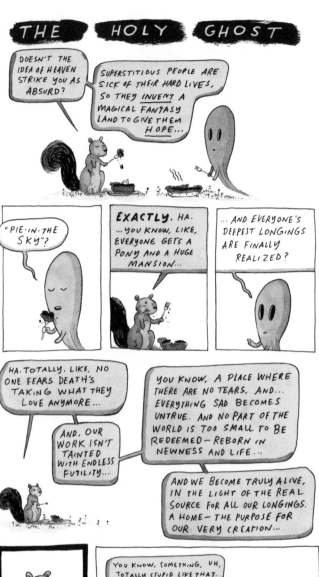

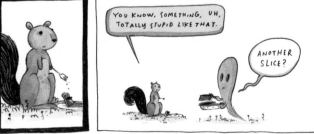

The Holy Ghost

TIME IS GOD'S CREATURE, NOT HIS REALITY.

HE LIVES OUTSIDE ITS LIMITS— LIKE AN AUTHOR LIVES OUTSIDE HIS STORY.

BUT THE OPPOSITE OF LINEAR TIME IS NOT INFINITY, BUT SINGULARITY— ALL TIME AT ONCE.

WE IMAGINE HEAVEN AS UNENDING HAPPINESS, BUT PERHAPS IT IS MORE LIKE BEING ENCASED IN ALL OF GOD'S GOODNESS AT ONCE... IN A SINGLE FOREVER-NOW.

THE JOYULARITY.

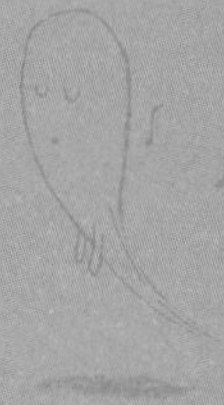

THE HOLY GHOST

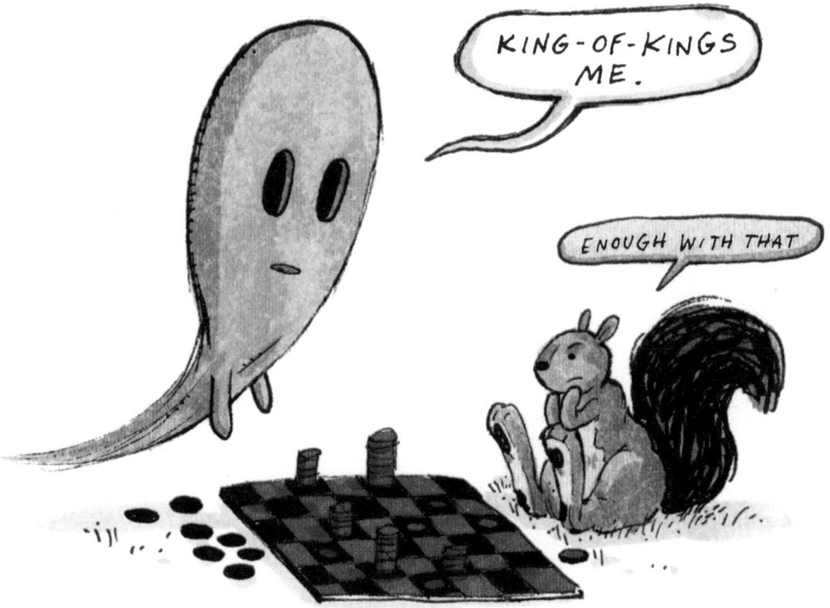
KING-OF-KINGS ME.
ENOUGH WITH THAT

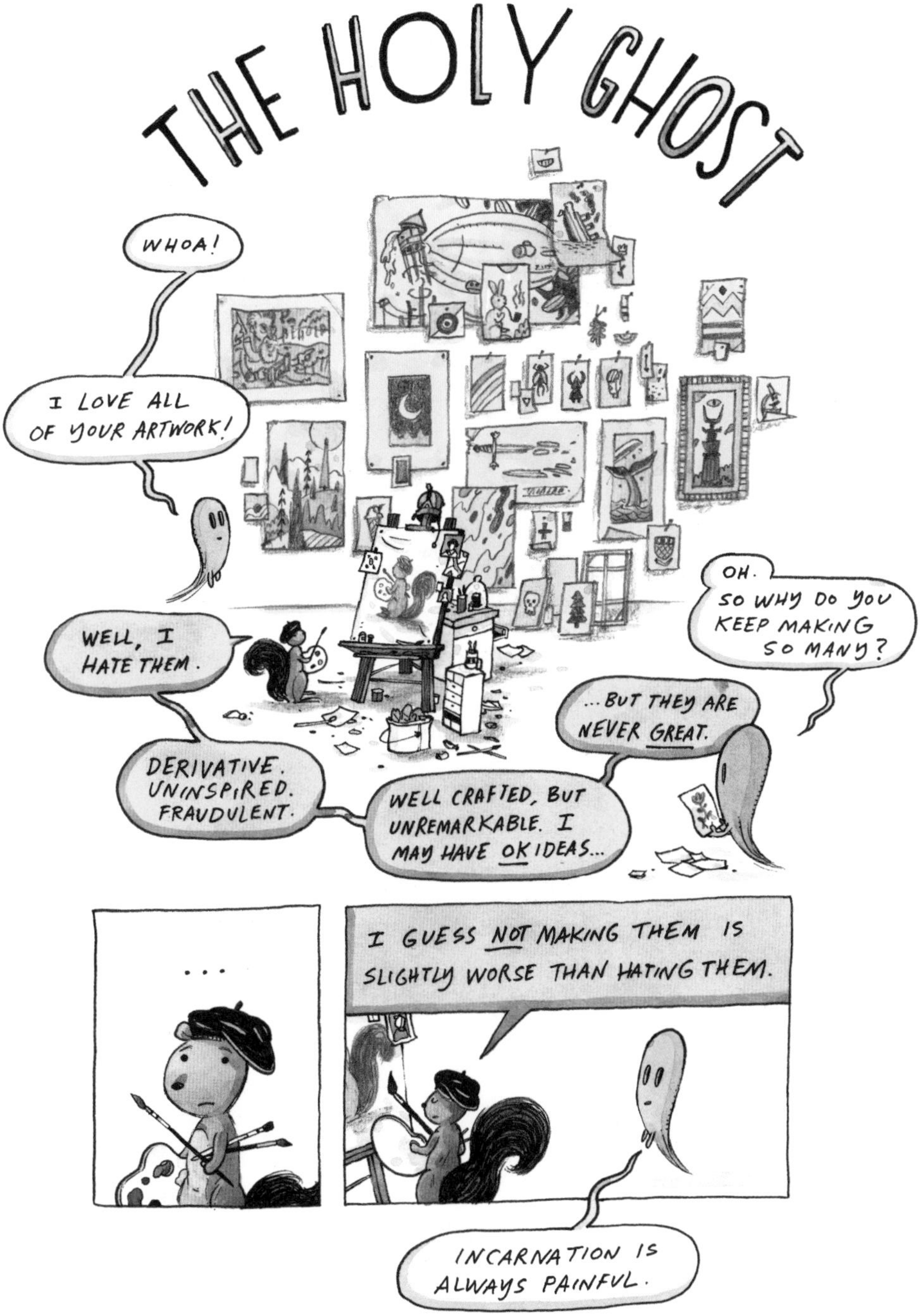
THE HOLY GHOST
WHOA!
I LOVE ALL OF YOUR ARTWORK!
WELL, I HATE THEM.
DERIVATIVE. UNINSPIRED. FRAUDULENT.
WELL CRAFTED, BUT UNREMARKABLE. I MAY HAVE OK IDEAS...
...BUT THEY ARE NEVER GREAT.
OH. SO WHY DO YOU KEEP MAKING SO MANY?
. . .
I GUESS NOT MAKING THEM IS SLIGHTLY WORSE THAN HATING THEM.
INCARNATION IS ALWAYS PAINFUL.

THE HOLY GHOST

SOB
OH GOD...
WHERE ARE YOU? GOD!?
WHY... GOD...
DO YOU DISAPPEAR IN TIMES OF TROUBLE?!
SOB
WHY HIDE YOURSELF?
SOB
...SNIFF...
GOD?
...SNIFF...
...ZZZZ
I'M STILL HERE.

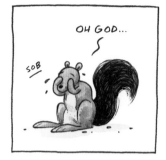

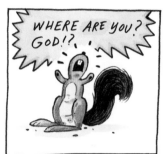

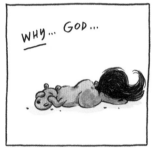

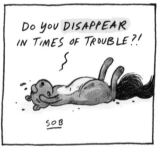

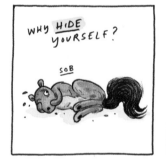

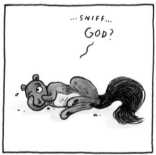

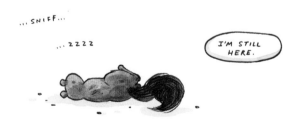

THE HOLY GHOST

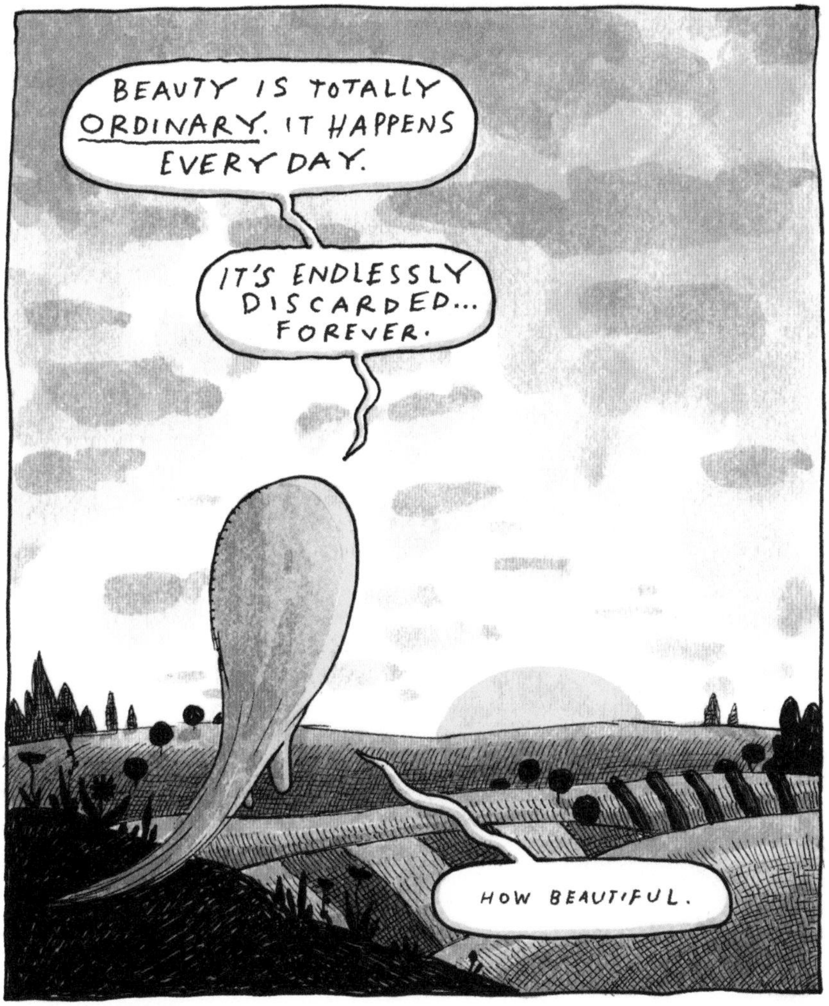
BEAUTY IS TOTALLY ORDINARY. IT HAPPENS EVERY DAY.
IT'S ENDLESSLY DISCARDED... FOREVER.
HOW BEAUTIFUL.

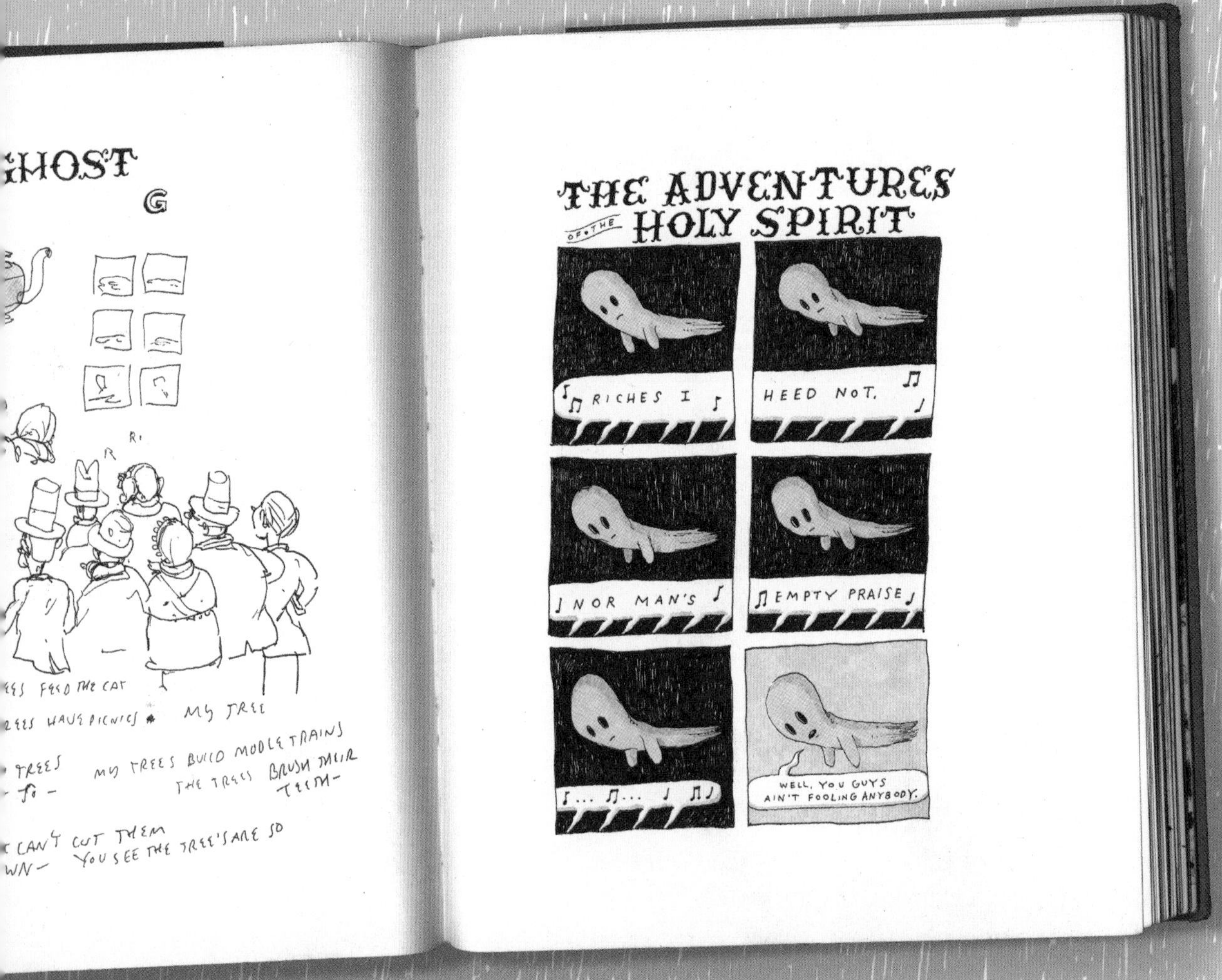
GHOST
THE ADVENTURES OF THE HOLY SPIRIT
RICHES I
HEED NOT.
NOR MAN'S
EMPTY PRAISE
WELL, YOU GUYS AIN'T FOOLING ANYBODY.
MY TREE
MY TREES BUILD MODLE TRAINS
THE TREES BRUSH THEIR TEETH—
YOU SEE THE TREE'S ARE SO

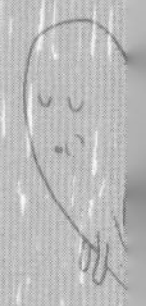

Sketchbook spread, 2012. First appearance of the comic *The Holy Ghost.*

AUTHOR'S NOTE

It started ten years ago. I was sitting in church, listening to a sermon, which is just another way of saying that I was drawing. The message that day, delivered by my pastor, the late and dear Kurt Lutjens, was on the enigmatic nature of the trinity. Although I don't recall the exact details of the message, I do remember entering a feeling of numinous wonder. As my ruminations processed through the visual side of my brain, I was struck by how little material I had to work with. It seemed that my visual language had not fully explored the literal form of the trinity, and especially that of the Holy Ghost.

I don't really know what I think until I start drawing. I took a stab at a comic based on a hymn we were singing that day in church, "Be Thou My Vision," and I imagined a literal blue ghost listening, hovering above the congregation. The little comic delighted me beyond words. But more than charming me, I was suddenly able to see something that was previously unseeable. All image making is incarnating. The collision of words and images together conveys something new, a third language that neither can do alone.

The Holy Ghost, as a piece of Christian theology revealed in the New Testament, is taught as both a mystery and the very device that unlocks that mystery. In a small way, this comic was a way for me to participate in the riddle. What started as a side project that initially lived in my sketchbook slowly turned into a small obsession. I was thinking about comic ideas all the time, and stealing time away from "actual work" to make these comics for fun. Eventually the process became more intentional and designed. In the early days, I would not even draft the dialogue. But as the voice of the characters became clearer, I would spend hours honing the economy of the language and drawing multiple drafts of the layout.

Despite the increasing investment in these characters, I'm more bashful about this book than any other work I've published. Firstly, because I never fully envisioned these being collected together in a format like this. Secondly, because they are deeply personal. What began as visual rumination quickly turned into a spiritual diary. I do not understand faith without doubt. The laments and questions in these comics are my own. They are not meant as informational tracts to illustrate theology (though for some that may be an outcome). Rather, they are expressions of a mind wrestling with the alternating seasons of faith and doubt

that are familiar to any person of faith, no matter the belief system. The comics became a way to preach to myself over many years and many seasons of life. These are not published in order of creation, but have been arranged for thematic rhythm and variety. The visual style of the characters changed over the years, as it often does with comics. Some were made in church in my sketchbook, others while I was crammed into a bumpy middle seat on a plane, and others on my quiet drafting table in the studio.

Though I am taking some semi-irreverent liberties with the trinity, I would like to state in clear terms that I am not positing that the Holy Ghost is a literal blue ghost. My goals were never to make any kind of dogmatic statements about Christian theology. As the musician Rich Mullins said, "We were given the Scriptures to humble us into realizing that God is right, and the rest of us are just guessing." When the comics in this collection are at their best they ask questions more than suggest firm answers. My hope is that, no matter your disposition on Christian theology, these comics can make you smile, and remind you of those questions you forgot you once had.

ACKNOWLEDGMENTS

It would be impossible for any student of the field of comics not to see the debt I owe to Bill Watterson and Charles Schultz. In a single conversation between a child and a stuffed tiger, Watterson could deftly move from the prosaic to the profound. As for *Peanuts*, Schultz gave to the world a daily gift of characters that were able to wrestle with both melancholy and hope, all in three or four panels at a time. Both of these masterwork collections are the true rosetta stone of the material explored in this book.

I must credit the C. S. Lewis book *The Screwtape Letters*, which I first read as a teenager and have since reread many times. It gave me my first picture of imaginative, thoughtful, and hilarious theology. I would like to thank Brad Lewis for being my first reader for many of these comics in recent years. Once I began drafting them, before the final drawing, he became an invaluable editor. Somehow this gifted lawyer always took the time to look through a draft of a comic on his phone at a moment's notice. Huge thanks to my faithful editor, Howard Reeves, who quickly improved many of these comics. Thank you to Abrams Books. I'm grateful to have a publishing team that trusts me enough to invest in a book of comics exploring ideas of faith and Christian theology.

To Jack, Annie, Garry (and Chippy)

The illustrations in this book were created by hand with micron pens on Strathmore 400 Series paper. Most of the images were colored with fluid acrylic paints, but some were colored digitally on a Wacom Cintiq drawing tablet. The text is set in Strada, Whitney, and a custom typeface based on my handwriting, built by John Martz. Some of these comics were colored by my studio assistant Annie Hendrix.

Editor: Howard W. Reeves
Designer: Pamela Notarantoio
Managing Editor: Marie Oishi
Production Manager: Alison Gervais

Library of Congress Cataloging Number 2021945015

ISBN 978-1-4197-5543-9

Printed and bound in China

10 9 8 7 6 5 4 3 2 1

Abrams ComicArts books are available at special discounts when purchased in quantity for premiums and promotions as well as fundraising or educational use. Special editions can also be created to specification. For details, contact specialsales@abramsbooks.com or the address below.

Abrams ComicArts® is a registered trademark of Harry N. Abrams, Inc.

ABRAMS The Art of Books
195 Broadway, New York, NY 10007
abramsbooks.com